Making It: 40 & Beyond

Making It: 40 & Beyond

Davitz & Davitz

Winston Press

Library of Congress Catalog Card Number: 79-63230

ISBN: 0-03-051561-0

Winston Press, Inc.
430 Oak Grove
Minneapolis, MN 55403

Printed in the United States of America
5   4   3   2

To know
That which before us lies in daily life
Is prime wisdom.
                    —*JOHN MILTON*

acknowledgments

Throughout this book, many different people living through the decade of their forties speak for themselves. They shared experiences with us, discussing their lives from forty to fifty. We should like to express our deepest appreciation, respect and gratitude for their time and interest in our work.

L.D.

J.D.

contents

Middle Forties

Late Forties

part three / HER

Early Forties

Middle Forties

Making It: 40 & Beyond

introduction

For an American in the twentieth century, leaving thirty-nine and becoming forty represents a huge leap in the process of aging, a leap that can be both critical and painful. The reasons for the crisis and pain almost never have anything to do with the physical process of aging. In fact, just before or just after one's fortieth birthday, there are no physical changes worth noting whatever. But there are changes—and real ones, most of which are the result of the very dramatic way in which this culture defines life "after forty," and the equally dramatic way in which we respond to that definition.

We began this study of life after forty because of our interest in the problems many people meet at this stage of adulthood. But over and over again, despite the many problems discussed, we were struck by the fact that these problems were often the springboard for psychological development. Gradually, we came to realize that in the long run, the stresses of the post-forty years are less important than the ways in which people react to them. And we also learned that the nature of these reactions depends to a certain extent on an individual's self-understanding. By sharing the experiences of others, learning from the thoughts and feelings of those who have lived through the post-forty years, each of us can gain greater understanding of our own lives, and on the basis of this "prime wisdom," fulfill the promise of our maturity.

Aging is both a physical and a sociopsychological phenomenon. Physically everyone ages from the moment life begins. It is a continuous process with gradual changes throughout the life span. But from a sociopsychological point of view we tend to think of aging in terms of points that mark the end of one stage and the beginning of another. Learning to speak, for instance, signifies a move from infancy to early childhood. Other points are marked by the beginning of certain activities: starting school or graduating from college. Certain civil and legal responsibilities can identify part of the process of aging. But there seems to be no aging quite so profoundly devastating in this country as entering the forties.

At other times in history and in other cultures, the ages signifying the beginning of maturity vary—some are much earlier than forty, some much later. But for Americans and most Europeans, there is a clear and decisive shift in the perspective of the individual and the way others view us at forty. We are no longer young adults, fresh, light-hearted, buoyant. We are now experienced, settled, with increasing difficulties in identifying with youth and youthfulness. Our concern is whether we are "over the hill," a man or woman of maturity approaching portly or matronly middle age.

It is precisely because of these cultural and psychological influences that the years from forty to fifty are probably the most misunderstood decade in life. Analyses of these years run the gamut from "Life really begins at forty" to "You don't have to be forty at all; you can be eternally twenty-seven." In both extremes, the obvious point is that one can and should alter or avoid the forties at whatever costs. For it is a deadly decade, dull, lifeless, and wholly without a future that is worth living out.

In actual fact, other than the first ten years of life, no other decade is more intriguing, complex, interesting, and unsettled. Its characteristics are change, flux, crisis, growth, and intense challenges. Other than childhood, no period has a greater impact on the balance of our lives, for at no other time is anxiety coupled with so great a possibility for fulfill-ment.

The anxiety which usually accompanies entrance into the decade of the forties frequently appears to be the result of being pushed and pulled by incomprehensible forces. There is a sense of being overwhelmed by mysterious internal and external forces. The principal question, of course, is, What can we do about the anxiety? and How can we get on to the fulfillment? In our culture, having been taught that there is a "cure" for every unpleasantness, we naturally look for the drugstore or guru to give us something that will make every-thing all right again. To be perfectly honest, there is no magic cure, and we are not willing to recommend placebos or indulge ourselves with fantasy. Cotton candy promises are designed for placating children. No placebo, no trip to Ber-muda, or Madeira, no evening gown or sports jacket will solve the very real problems of living through the forties. At forty we are as close to adulthood as we will ever be, and as adults talking to adults, we can admit the truth: some things require personal confrontation, a willingness to get to and through a situation without a sugar-coated pill. We cannot offer simple, guaranteed techniques to short-circuit the crisis of the forties.

This is not to say there are no weapons, no ways of coping. There are. And it is our hope that they are clearly illustrated by the people who speak in this book. First of all, there is knowledge. Knowledge is itself the greatest weapon, for it provides a rational basis for responding to problems with confidence. When we know enough to identify a phase of our development we are just that much better able to handle it when it appears.

Second, there is tolerance. For both men and women, the period between forty and fifty involves growth through trial and error, trying out different activities, interests, and per-spectives. It is a time for experimentation and change. We should therefore anticipate and tolerate, in ourselves and in others, ambiguity, confusion, doubt, and mistakes. In a way they are the price we pay for the opportunity to develop psychologically. The important point is not to be afraid of these changes, this doubt, and this experimentation. Even more important is remembering that confronting a crisis is a way of growing.

Another means of handling this period of life is communication. Verbalizing our concerns presents a special problem during the forties because relationships with significant "others"—those with whom communication has been most intimate and meaningful in the past—may be seriously disrupted. But every effort should be made to keep these channels of communication open, even if the messages getting through are hostile ones. It is far better to keep communicating with significant others, though the communications may entail some fighting, than to withdraw behind walls of silence.

Also, since the behavioral extremes are pronounced during this period, it is extremely important to exercise some caution. Major decisions should be weighed very carefully, certainly as carefully as the decisions of childhood are weighed by parents.

Last is perhaps the single most important thing to remember. The years from forty to fifty are developmental. That is, they have a beginning, a middle, and happily an end. When we are in the midst of suffering a psychological crisis we may feel hopelessly trapped and depressed because we believe that our problems will go on endlessly. These feelings are real and neither can nor should be dismissed. Nevertheless, knowing that such stresses will be eased eventually and the problems will somehow be resolved can give us the necessary support we need when we are in the depths of depression. For at the "end" of this decade lies the promise of genuine personal growth. If the crises of the forties are viewed from this perspective, this is the one single promise that can be abundantly fulfilled.

As we talked with some two hundred persons who were actually experiencing some phase of the forties (and no one has *all* of the problems described here) we became convinced that perspective was vital. If the forties are viewed only as a time of threat and stress they will be experienced that way. If we learn to stand back a bit we are much more likely to be able to employ the weapons available to us for coping.

As the personal narratives that follow show, there are striking differences between the way men respond to certain pressures and the way these pressures affect women. The book, therefore, has a part entitled *Him* and one entitled *Her*. But because the impact of certain general problems is irrespective of sex, the first part, *We*, is directed to the experiences and stresses that men and women have in common during the years from forty to fifty. The subdivisions of Parts Two and Three—Early Forties, Middle Forties and Late Forties—not only indicate the very marked differences among these three phases of forty to fifty, but reveal the developmental aspect of the period. In the conversations with our interviewees, our strongest delight was witnessing the consistent expressions of growth, of having reached a level of fulfillment, of emotional freedom that had no precedent in the earlier years. They had, in fact, *achieved* fifty, and were experiencing a genuine personal renaissance.

For this edition of *Making It: 40 and Beyond,* we have prepared, with Roger J. Radley, twenty exercises in personal growth.

These exercises, found in the Appendix, are designed to help you reflect upon your own life experience and the life experience of others. You can complete the exercises by yourself, but you may wish to share them with another person or a group of people.

However you choose to do the exercises, they are important, for life beyond forty is not merely something to read about; it is meant to be lived thoroughly and productively.

part one

WE

Intimations of Mortality

"You read column after column of people who died."

All men are mortal.
Socrates is a man.
Therefore, Socrates is mortal.

That simple syllogism is used to illustrate elementary logic, but within the syllogism lies the core of a profound problem in our psycho-logic. We all know the syllogism, and have probably read or said it a number of times. But we have rarely if ever thought that our own name could be substituted for "Socrates," and if it has occurred to us, we really haven't taken the possibility very seriously.

Therefore, when glancing through a newspaper we happen to notice that someone we went to school with has just died—someone our own age—we merely note it in passing, perhaps mention the fact to our husband or wife, but it creates barely a ripple on the surface of our everyday life. We believe we have forgotten it. Then one day, like a forty-one-year-old sales representative for a large advertising firm, we realize that we are actually interested in the obituary columns.

When I was a kid I used to see my father reading obituary pages. I wondered about it. Sometimes he'd even read obituaries aloud. People he never knew. He'd

shake his head and say, "Poor guy off for a last ride."
I thought to myself what difference did it make to him
that some guy he never knew had a heart attack.

I don't wonder any more about his habit. I found
myself doing the same thing. It's a strange compulsion.
You read column after column of people who died.
And then you compare ages. You feel lucky when you
read about someone younger. I'm convinced it's self-
torture. I wonder if other people read them. They
must, otherwise why would newspapers have a whole
page of these notices?

Every now and then I come across a name of someone who I know. It happened to me recently. There
was a whole column about this fellow who I sort of
remember in college. We didn't really know each other
well. But the notice bothered me. Thought maybe I'd
send a card to the family. I cut the obit out and put
it in my pocket. Would you believe it? The next few
days I walked around feeling dragged down. Someone
asked me what was wrong. I said, "An old college
buddy died." What a liar. I didn't know that guy that
well. I never sent the card and I threw away the clip-
ping.

We find ourselves scanning the obituary page more
and more often, briefly but distinctly noting the ages of
those who died yesterday. Not many forty-year-olds make
the page, but a few do show up, and unconsciously we
begin a tabulation. As time passes there is another—and
another—and another. Then, one day, it's not a stranger
—it's someone we know, someone we saw yesterday,
played golf with last weekend, were going to meet for
lunch next Thursday. And the shock of loss is amplified
by our awareness that if people we know can be substituted for Socrates in the old syllogism, so too can our
own name. It is no longer an abstract exercise in logic; it

is a fact of our own life—and our own inevitable death.

An orthodontist, forty-one years of age, commented on precisely these facts of life and how his attitudes had undergone a marked change in recent months.

I can't remember thinking much about death when I was a kid. Sure people died. I went to my grandparents' funerals, but that's about the sum of it. People died— other people—not me. It was like a TV show or a movie. Bodies could drop all over the place. Someone always getting murdered—dying—all part of a show. You don't look at the body on the screen being buried and say to yourself, "That could be me." Someone else is doing the dying.

It's only lately as I get older that it hits me that maybe I could die. It wouldn't be a show. It would be real. It was a crazy feeling thinking that way. I was out playing ball with my son and we were having a great time and suddenly it crossed my mind, "What would happen to him if I died? How would my wife manage?" I got tight inside worrying. I didn't want to die. I wanted to see him grow up. I was using him as my excuse to stay alive. It's not as if I were sick or anything but you don't have to be sick to die. What I mean is it could come without warning. You could go in a plane crash, an accident on the road. I kept thinking about it for a while—really bothered me. I felt I had to stay alive for the family. I'm at that age when I hear of friends dying of heart attacks. It makes me think. I say to myself, OK, you're forty-two. You've reached the halfway mark. You're on the way down to the goal line. Perhaps that's what separates kids from adults. You know you're grown up the day you realize there's no second time around. You've only got so much time in this life.

The awareness of death is reenforced when we visit a friend hospitalized with bleeding ulcers or for a heart condition. Our own heart may be in fine shape, and we may never have had the slightest suggestion of an ulcer but people do die from heart attacks or from hemorrhaging ulcers—people, that is, in their early forties. Thus, we need not be a master logician to revise the syllogism and conclude that "I, too, am mortal," and we can understand perfectly the anxiety of this forty-two-year-old part owner of an import-export firm who reacted to his partner's sudden hospitalization with fear and concern, not only for his friend, but for himself. Both of the men had enjoyed excellent health. In fact, only a week before, they had played their customary eighteen holes of golf.

My partner and I had been working day and night on a promotional campaign. I get a telephone call from his wife. John is in the hospital, she tells me. She was hysterical. I went over to the hospital. She tells me that he came in at two in the morning and they sat down for coffee and he keeled over with a heart attack. I had this feeling she blamed me. We both worked hard. It could have been me. But you can't reason with someone at a time like this.

I was disturbed. John never seemed like a heart trouble candidate. He was athletic, didn't smoke, or drink much. It was a week before he could have visitors. I was thrown when I saw him. My face must have shown something.

"I look pretty bad?" he asks me. I told him to stop feeling sorry for himself, that all he wanted was a vacation because we were busy in the office. You kid around in situations like that. What could I tell him—that he looked like hell? His face was drained. His cheeks caved in and he was white as a sheet.

I stayed maybe a half an hour. "You look fine; you'll

be up and around in a week; take it easy; I can manage
without you; you'll make up the work when you get
back." You should have heard the list of crap I handed
out. I left feeling rotten inside. It's downhill for John.
I'm no doctor, but it didn't take much to know he was
in bad shape. And I kept telling myself, John is forty-
two and I'm forty-three. His illness set me back.
What's it all for anyhow, I asked myself, if you end up
flat on your back with medicine pumped into your arm
and machines standing over you?

Members of the "Older" Generation

*"For the first time I faced the fact that I was
another age; I belonged to another generation."*

Aware of our own mortality, increasingly sensitive to everyday aches, pains, and feelings of fatigue, we begin to worry
more and more about minor ills, and we are distressed by the
fact that it takes longer and longer to recuperate from
strenuous exertion, colds, muscle strains, headaches, and
hangovers. The possibility of a major illness becomes a major
concern.

At work we begin to suspect that we will not reach the
pinnacle of success that has been our goal for so many years.
Frustrated and threatened, we experience self-doubt and
become especially sensitive to any sign that others may be
losing confidence in us. We are no longer a young man or
woman on the way up, and people no longer react to us in
that role. Younger people, especially, see us differently from

the way we see ourselves, and we probably react to this discovery with some consternation, as did the forty-one-year-old woman who reported the following incident.

You go along thinking you haven't gotten any older, and then someone says something, and you get caught up short. I know for a fact that I personally think I am youngish and attractive. Lots of people tell me how nice I look. I don't feel "past forty," whatever that means.

I did get a setback though, when I was down at my husband's office and I was in the coffee shop with some of the young clerks. One of them was very sweet, and then she asked me if I had been married very long. I told her I had been married twenty years. She was shocked and then she said to me, "You look very nice for a woman your age." I knew she wasn't trying to be mean or anything like that, but the way her words came out was a setback for me. I realized for the first time girls her age see me quite differently from the way I see myself in a mirror. The reflection I see hasn't aged. For those young girls I was "over the hill." Her words really bothered me. I thought about them a lot the next weeks.

From a social point of view, one's age is defined partly by the other people with whom one is associated or classified. A thirty-year-old is defined as a young adult partly by the fact that others see her as a member of an age group of young adults. It may come as something of a shock to learn that younger women no longer see her as one of their own age group, but rather as one of an older generation. A forty-two-year-old social worker described such an experience.

I may not feel my age, but other people sure aren't going to let me forget. It's little comments that bother me. I was at lunch with the staff yesterday, and I said something or other, and a couple of girls said that's exactly what their mothers would have said. At the time I hadn't felt an age difference between us. Being compared with their mothers caught me up short. Then I remember that one of the other women whom I see as really fortyish always talks to me about how women our age see things differently from the younger staff. I get resentful. I want to tell her she may be thinking and feeling forty-plus, but I am not ready to fold my hands and rock away the years. I know she doesn't mean anything, though it bothers me the way she sets women our age off in a separate group.

Gradually we become a "senior person" at the office, a person due a certain amount of respect and deference, not always because of our personal power, but because of age and seniority. It was this insight that was most disturbing to a forty-three-year-old assistant manager of the sales division of a large corporation.

I was brought up in the old school. Work hard and you got it made. You can't miss. So what does it get you? I've found out. I've been with my company for twenty-two years. Sure, I've had promotions, salary increases. Let me tell you, if it weren't for me there wouldn't be a sales division. I was riding high—feeling good about myself and where I was going. I had some ideas for a new push.

Then it all turned. It's like I was walking on a street I knew like the back of my hand. I come to a corner and someone changed the street signs.

I was at the office. We have a water cooler in the corridor. I went out and filled a paper cup and just stood there drinking the water, and the elevator door opened. Out comes one of the vice-presidents with a young guy next to him. He greets me and we talk and he turns and tells this kid, "Want you to meet Bob Henning, one of our steady hands in sales." He grabs my shoulder and says, "People like Bob are rocks around here. Firm couldn't get along without our old steadies."

That afternoon our division gets an announcement about a new manager. That kid. You know, I sat there with that memo and I kept hearing "old steady" pounding in my head. I had a job, a place in the executives' dining room. Passed over for a kid—maybe thirty. Takes the wind out of you. Twenty-two years, and all you got to show for it is a clap on the back and "old steady." I asked myself, "Where the hell was I going all those years?"

At meetings, colleagues sometimes ask him how something used to be done; he is one of those asked to put things into historical perspective—and even when he is not asked, he occasionally finds himself thinking about the ways things used to be around the office.

A professor in the history department of a university spoke about how he felt as the senior man. The realization of the temporal quality of his role bothered him after an encounter with younger faculty members.

We had our first faculty meeting with junior staff members—lecturers, instructors, and assistant professors. I mentioned Professor Thomas several times. You have to appreciate that for over twenty-five years Professor Thomas was a dean around here—one of the big names on campus. He retired seven years ago.

The first question I was asked was "Who was Professor Thomas?" What do I say? I looked at that instructor. Then others asked the same thing. "Who was Professor Thomas?"

You know, for the first time I faced the fact I was another age; I belonged to another generation. I was a senior man in the department. I studied under Thomas. He ran this place since I was a graduate student. And now, seven years after he leaves, people ask who he was. Forgotten—someone who spent twenty-five years—forgotten. It pulled me up short. I was in a different world. I had moved into a new position. You're up there in the senior ranks for a while, then retire, and the next people move in and couldn't care less.

I had the same feeling when I brought home a recording of an old singer I remembered from college. My son never heard of her. Years ago people slept on sidewalks to be sure to get a ticket for her concert. You have one thing like this and then another happening, and you begin to realize that you're becoming history —dead history for the under forties.

He's certainly not finished yet—there are plenty of solid, productive years left—but when there is a new and especially challenging problem, people don't automatically turn to him. Although at first he is resentful, and may become irritated and perhaps angry, he also breathes a sigh of relief —to himself, of course, and very quietly, perhaps even while he is expressing his annoyance about not being consulted.

The Question of Identity

"Who have I been?"

The major psychological consequence of this growing system of stress is repetition of a crisis we faced when we were young—the identity crisis. But now the questions that lie at the heart of this crisis take a markedly different form. In late adolescence and early adult life, the question was "Who am I?" We were in the throes of defining ourselves as adults in an adult world. Obviously, this was not our first attempt to define ourselves as people. We began the process of self-definition in early infancy, and throughout our childhood and early adolescence an increasingly distinctive sense of self gradually emerged. But in later adolescence, this phase of our development came to a head. It became our major psychological focus, the prime motivating force of much of our behavior. And the answer to our question "Who *am* I?" —an answer painfully forged in the crucible of our late teens and early twenties—was the identity we lived with during the next twenty or so years. In the early forties, identity again becomes the focus, but now it is characterized by the strain imposed by a budding system of stresses, threats, frustrations, and fears.

Our central question is no longer "Who am I?" Putting the question in the present tense doesn't work, for now we have a history and are increasingly concerned about our future. Having recognized the fact of our own mortality, we become powerfully aware of the average span of a lifetime and believe that we have one last chance to make a significant difference in our lives. We now ask a very complex set of interrelated questions: *Who have I been? Who have I become? Who will I be?* -

We take a *Janus* stance—looking both to the past and to the future. We begin to question the wisdom, the validity, the values of the earlier identity crisis we resolved years before. "Did I choose the kind of work that permits the fullest realization of my potential? Did I marry the person with whom I can achieve the deepest love of which I am capable? Did I pledge my allegiance to the values and beliefs, the way of life that will lead to true fulfillment of my self?"

. These questions take on added emotional force when we . realize that the answers we furnish now will be the answers we must live with for the rest of our lives. A forty-two-year-old owner of a wholesale appliance distributing company sensed a growing boredom with and indifference to the routines of his work. And his questions involve both an appraisal and doubt concerning his past, his present, and his future.

My father insisted I take over the business. It seemed a good deal. He wanted to retire. He had built up the business. He said to me it was all mine and I could go ahead and do what I wanted. I first said no but changed my mind. After all, what did I have to lose? I had security. I still could do what I wanted in my free time. Why throw over a good business? I can't complain. The business has expanded. Financially I'm set, but year after year the same routine makes me wonder. Maybe I'm not like my father. He loved the business. He would come home when I was a kid and all he could think and talk about was business. Me—maybe I'm different. I get this feeling the business owns my life. Sometimes I feel like going over to the file drawers of paper and shredding them all in the wastebasket. I pick up letters the secretary writes and I want to set a match to them. It's the same damn thing day after day. An in-basket and an out-basket—in and out. I shift papers around. The other day we had a company meeting. I was listening to one of the men making a report. When

he finished I realized I hadn't heard one damn word he
said—and what's more, I didn't care.

Not every person consciously formulates the questions of
identity precisely as stated here. *Who have I been? Who
have I become? Who will I be?* These questions take idiosyn-
cratic forms. For some of us the crisis may be faced largely
on a conscious level, with more or less clear awareness of the
issues of identity that are being confronted. For others, the
bulk of the crisis may occur at an unconscious level, with
little awareness of the developmental problems that are being lived through. Regardless of the level of our awareness
or the degree to which our responses to the issues are conscious or unconscious, these questions of past, present, and
future identity define the central psychological crisis we face
in the early years of this troubled and troubling decade of
life.

The Discomfited Past

*"The worst part is I'll never know what might have
been."*

The resolution of our initial identity crisis in late adolescence and early adulthood depended, in part, on developing
a sense of values, an ideology to which we could feel genu-
inely committed. For most people, this does not involve a
formal and systematic statement of The Good, The Beautiful, and The True. Rather, it is a more or less consistent but
often vague and unspoken point of view from which life is
seen and experienced, an implicit framework within which

the events of living are understood and evaluated.

As this identity is threatened, we become increasingly concerned with this implicit ideology, with the beliefs, values, attitudes, and goals that have been the psychological framework of our day-to-day life for so many years. At this level of our development, there is often nothing we can pinpoint as wrong, inadequate, invalid. There is merely a vague sense of dissatisfaction, of something askew, which is typically accompanied by more frequent remembrances of things past, particularly those events and experiences that were crucial to our way of life. We may be ambivalent about these experiences, not able to identify the nature of the conflict. Our reflections may take a philosophical turn toward questions of meaning and value, but they may be blocked by an obsessive repetition of vague questions symptomatic of our discomfort. In one form or another, we ask ourselves over and over again, "What is the meaning of it all?" But being trapped by a network of obsessions, we are unable to move on from feeling discomfort with our past to new possibilities for our future.

A forty-three-year-old owner of an art supplies and picture framing store spoke about his son's career, his doubts, and his own struggles in adolescence.

My son wants to become a professional singer. Caruso he's not. Sinatra he'll never be. He's talented but not first-rate. I'm not kidding him or myself. I tried to tell him why knock yourself out studying, wasting years on a minor talent? You have so much going for you, I told him.

He said he'll find out himself if he isn't any good. If he doesn't at least try he'll never know. I hate to see him batting his head against a wall, wasting a few years he can't recapture. He should keep singing as a hobby, an outlet, but not as a life career. He is going ahead anyhow. He asked me if I would at least give him the money I would have spent on his college.

Maybe he's right. Maybe he has to get it out of his system. Maybe I'm envious. I didn't dare do what he is doing at his age. I had ideas of becoming an artist. I had successes, a few prizes, honors—the same as he has had in singing. But I let my parents convince me it wouldn't be a career. I could never support a family with a paintbrush—that's what was drummed into me. I didn't go ahead.

I took the safe way, and it's been a good life. I don't regret my decision, except maybe now. When I see my past repeating itself in my son, I wonder. What if I had tried? Would there have been a chance? Would I have made it? I never tried, so I'll never know. Years for me can't be turned back. The worst part is I'll never know what might have been.

The brooding melancholy of this period is neither pleasant nor pleasurable; yet, the experience of crisis seems to add a new dimension, a greater depth to our emotional life. In our middle and late thirties, our emotional reactions were clear, strong, and sometimes blaring. But when we enter the forties, we discover a greater range of emotional reaction, a finer sensitivity, a deeper timbre in the tone of our inner life. It is becoming more complex, fuller, and more resonant. Quietly, without fanfare, we are becoming emotionally richer, more mature and interesting human beings.

Although we are becoming more interesting, dynamic, complex people, we are not very pleasant or amusing. As our sense of personal crisis deepens and grows, we become increasingly egocentric—we focus on *our* identity, *our* problems, *our* aches, *our* death, *our* future. We are irritable, touchy, explosive, yet also gentler, at times, in our relationships with others. In short, we are in the throes of a crucial stage in psychological development, a time fraught with frustration, aggression, and despair, but also a time of new possibilities, new growth, and a fuller realization of human potential.

part two

HIM

early forties

The Rumblings of Crisis

*"I get the feeling the world is pulling apart
at the seams."*

The average man leaves thirty-nine and becomes forty on a
wavecrest of energy, activity, and ambition. The plans he
made in his early and middle thirties are beginning to mature; the basic skills of his craft have been polished and
refined; there is a sense of power, movement, growth, and
dynamic thrust.

As he nears his fortieth birthday, he may feel a twinge of
apprehension, a moment of doubt. But these doubts are
mostly flashes of anecdotes about others who have passed
into this middle decade. Although the stories—amusing,
sometimes pathetic—are common, he is confident that "it
can't happen to me." He is full of life, energy, and power,
and is quite sure that the adolescent-like moping or the
escapades of some older friends are not part of his own
future. There is work to be done, ambition to stretch his
reach, and after the immature stumblings of his early adulthood, he finally has position, power, and skills.

This belief is reenforced by the fact that his daily life
continues in the same pattern of busy activity that characterized his late thirties. If anything, he is even more productive, more effective, and more substantially rewarded than
ever before. Dreams of his early twenties are almost within
reach. He feels that with one more burst of energy, another

stretch of himself, he will fulfill goals that began to form
many years before. At thirty-nine he sold a million dollars
worth of insurance. He thought of a great idea for a new
promotional campaign and pushed it through to success
with enthusiasm. He expanded his practice dramatically,
saw nearly twice as many people as he had five years earlier,
was doing a better job and making more money than ever
before. He had new ideas, plenty of talent, lots of energy;
he was clearly a young man on the way up—it was simply
a matter of time and opportunity, the right moment, the
right circumstances.

It didn't change much at forty. After a moment's brief
hesitation he continued his energetic upward climb, perhaps
with even renewed energy and renewed ambition. After all,
having come this far by forty, no need to set one's sights too
low—no need to settle for anything less than the very top.
This sense of renewed ambition is described by a successful
lawyer who recently became head of his firm after the death
of the senior partner.

I remember a course I had in college when a professor
talked about the ages of men in relationship to
creativity. A mathematician makes discoveries in his
early twenties. I'm not a mathematician and I wasn't
worried. I knew others who were. They became concerned because they didn't seem to be anywhere near
a great discovery. For most professions it takes time to
make your mark. There are geniuses who write sympho-
nies at twelve. A few writers hit the world with a book
at thirty—but these are exceptions.

The professor spoke about getting a stride as you
neared forty. I know what he means—I didn't know
then. You have to have some life experiences.

Know-how about the world takes time. In my profession, especially, a few gray hairs can't hurt. You need
them to give a client confidence. That's how I feel now

—people have confidence in me. I'm moving toward a peak and it feels good. People come to me; I don't have to hustle. When you start out—I don't care who you are—you have some hustling to do; a lunch here and there, a party to meet the right people.

Now I can unwind and let the calls come to me. Don't get me wrong. I'm not out for power. I made up my mind I wanted to be head of my own firm, and I wanted to have a damn good, honest firm. I was junior partner until our senior man died. I changed the brass plate on the door and got new stationery. I don't fool myself. I'm too much of a realist. I like my name first. I'm not where I want to be—not just yet. It's as if I can see my goal with one more move, one more push. Sometimes I feel, though, I'd like to have the present stand still—give me time to catch my second wind and enjoy the crest before the next wave comes my way.

Wives of men who have just turned forty are especially aware of this overwhelming energy. The thirty-five-year-old wife of the owner of a moderate-sized manufacturing concern spoke candidly about the frenzied pace of her husband, who had just celebrated his fortieth birthday.

We used to have time together. I could count on Saturdays and Sundays. But now he's running constantly. The business stays open an hour later, and he has books to do on the weekends. It's been weeks since we've been out—even to a neighborhood movie. It's me that's going crazy—locked in. I know he's working hard. What does he think I'm doing? I have the house and the children—but I am getting bored to death talking to children. I tell the kids, "Your father has to work late." They hardly ever see him. By the time he gets home we've had dinner, and they're in their rooms or in bed.

I've tried talking to him. He tells me I should feel lucky. He gets home at nine and some of the men he knows don't get home until later. And he reminds me sometimes he's home earlier. What good does that do? He has dinner late—then some TV, and he falls asleep in front of the set. I suppose I should feel grateful he's doing well.

But I'm scared with this constant running. Where will it end? So we won't have a million dollars. We wouldn't have a million if he worked all night. What good does money do anyhow? I don't need dress clothes if we never go anywhere. We haven't even time to have friends in. What does he want—more in the bank?

I remember meeting someone once, years ago—an old man. I was talking to a friend and saying that I didn't want to buy something because it cost too much. This old man tapped me on the shoulder. "Buy it," he told me. "There won't be pockets in your shroud." I never forgot what he said to me. You need only so much money, only so much success to be happy. I wish I knew what my husband wanted. Why he is driving himself? I ask myself, Where is it all going to end? We'll have money, but if we lose each other, the money won't make us happy.

Although life at forty continues at the active, hard-working pace of the previous decade, gradually the seams begin to weaken. No one can pinpoint the beginning; no one can say it was "there" or it was "then," because the change is a mixture, an interaction, a subtle and interwoven sequence of events. At first the momentary glimpse of a shadow, and then, without fanfare and without drama, in mundane everyday ways, the shadow becomes awareness. Not all at once, but with predictable inevitability, the man in his early forties begins to feel the same rumblings of a crisis in his life that a forty-two-year-old insurance executive, who has had a successful career in management, felt.

I read the newspapers, watch TV, listen to the radio, and I get the feeling the world is pulling apart at the seams, so maybe it's not just me feeling down. I look at people around me. How many do you see just laughing? People don't laugh like they used to. I remember as a kid, guys would get into the locker room and laugh. You know it wasn't always at someone—any little thing could set us off. We'd laugh. Now who laughs? I mean that seriously. Everything is responsibilities, work, jobs, the economy. One time I'd like to be in a situation where people just laugh. It sounds crazy. It's not. Maybe the truth is the reason people like myself aren't laughing is because there's nothing to laugh about, and worse—no one to laugh with.

The Signs of Ripening

"It got so I couldn't read the newspaper without falling asleep."

Awareness of mortality makes a man sensitive to the aches, pains, and ills that typically occur in a forty-year-old body. His speed, strength, and reaction time seem to be about the same, but he finds it takes longer to recover from strenuous exertion. If he plays two hours of tennis or twenty-seven holes of golf on Sunday, somehow he feels a bit more tired on Monday and Tuesday. Nothing serious, of course, since he remembers that even when he was thirty, he didn't feel much like running around the block after two hours of tennis. After all, he is not a professional athlete. Besides, he has other things to worry about more important than his physical condition—and two hours of tennis in one day is not bad at any age. But still and all, the slight edge of fatigue that lingers, the pulled muscle that takes longer to heal, the feeling in the morning of creaking bones are hints that his body is not getting any younger.

A nerve in a back tooth dies, and he has his first root-canal therapy—a miserable experience at any age, but at this time of life it's a painful sign of aging. Hangovers seem worse and last longer. Colds seem more debilitating, and he doesn't snap back as rapidly as he did when younger. He discovers the mysterious but real ache of the tennis elbow, charley horses come with surprisingly little strain, and his eyes, like those of a forty-one-year-old manager of a supermarket, tire sooner than they did in previous years. The idea of wearing glasses disturbed him so at first that he insisted he wore them only for reading; otherwise his eyes were perfect. He told about how he responded when he first became aware of his need.

It got so I couldn't read the newspaper without falling asleep. The letters jumped around on the page. My wife told me, "Why don't you get your eyes checked? Maybe you need glasses." I know people can wear glasses at any age. I see kindergarten kids with glasses. What you know and how you feel aren't the same.

I've always thought of myself as having a healthy body—a young body. I couldn't see myself with a paunch, diet lists, stomach ulcers—not me. The doctor said, "At your age you need glasses."

"Thanks, Doc"—what else do you say?

I tell you, it wasn't easy going out for that first pair of glasses. I went to this shop, and they must have let

out an old people's home. And me, what do I say to the
clerk? "They're only for reading. My eyes are good for
driving, just glasses for reading." What did he care? He
looks at me. I gave him a rough time. He couldn't
understand what was going on. And that was the start
of my saying to myself, O.K., join the ranks. You're on
the road downhill. So you get one pair, and then a few
years later, you get a stronger pair, then a hearing aid.
The whole bit. And that's how you know you're over
forty.

Music doesn't seem to have its usual richness as the man
in his early forties begins to lose sensitivity to sounds in the
higher frequencies. He may learn that his iron stomach that
could easily digest everything is gone; he may find his bowels
don't respond with regularity. The delights of a midafter-
noon nap on the weekends are discovered, and Saturday and
Sunday are more often devoted to rest and relaxation than
to running around town or doing extra work. He may have
trouble falling asleep, and he doesn't wake up each morning
feeling fresh and eager—even after a second cup of coffee.
His hair may be graying or thinning, and lack the spring of
earlier youth. Unwanted weight clings to his frame—and it
takes greater effort to lose it.

The wife of a forty-one-year-old account executive in a
stock brokerage house talked about how her husband reacted
when he became aware of a weight gain. Only in retrospect
had she realized why he became angry with her about a dry
cleaner.

My husband accused me of going to a cheap discount
cleaners who ruined his clothes. He insisted they used
a fluid which shrank all of his pants. It was true that
his trousers seemed shorter. But we have used the same
cleaners for years, and they are reliable. I told him I
would go back to the cleaners and complain. I know our

cleaning store. The owner said they hadn't changed products and had the latest equipment.

I wondered. My husband's clothes seemed tight. He has gained weight. I saw him standing in front of the bedroom mirror holding his breath in and pulling at the waist of his pants. He saw I was watching and became angry. He blamed me. Said that I made him get fat with the awful food I prepared. He always liked my cooking. It's never made him heavy before. I think he has cocktails at lunch and rich desserts. I told him he better not accuse me. His appetite is not my fault.

Another woman, wife of a department store manager in his early forties, described a recent family argument about her husband's concern over an obvious weight gain.

My husband asked me what was wrong with the bathroom scale. I told him nothing was wrong. He accused me of changing the dial and breaking it. I told him that was ridiculous. He went back to the scale, and I heard him moving it around the bathroom floor, getting on and off. I asked him what the matter was when he came out. He refused to answer directly. He told me he was throwing out the scale and buying a new one, that the old one was broken. I didn't dare tell him the scale was correct. The kids weighed themselves. They weighed the same as they did on the doctor's balance scale. I bought a new scale, and he told me I had bought a cheap one. I know he's definitely put on weight and doesn't want to admit it to himself.

Considered singly, none of these events may be very important. After all, we are always growing older, and always aware of some physical change. But during the early forties physical changes are likely to take on greater meaning than at other times, because then they have become part of a pattern of psychological aging, a pattern to which they contribute and which they also reenforce. To a man in his early forties, a charley horse is not only a sore muscle; it is the sign of a weakening body. Each petty illness, minor ache, spell of fatigue becomes the dreaded sign of ripening.

The Narrowing of Horizons

"Forget the dream. Keep the money at a safe six percent."

In addition to signs of ripening, the early-forties man begins to have problems in the world of work. A client for one reason or another decides not to renew his annual order — leaving a large gap in a sales manager's plan for the year. A professor who has been publishing in professional journals for over fifteen years has a paper rejected, with a brief note from the editor saying that the paper fails to meet journal standards. A lawyer loses a major case he was confident he could win. A dentist loses a few patients and discovers they have started seeing a young dentist who has just moved into the neighborhood. A promotion doesn't come through when expected; an advertising campaign isn't quite the hit it was supposed to be; a new idea is turned down; a patient who should have lived dies; a stock that should have gone up goes down; sales in a department are down from the same time last year—while other departments are up.

A forty-three-year-old Certified Public Accountant described his first professional setback. His competency was questioned for the first time since he had opened his office twenty years earlier.

I suppose I've been lucky. Never had my work questioned. Maybe that's why a setback I had six months ago still bothers me. You know, you handle my kind of detailed business for twenty years, and you have to know what you're doing. You can't be careless, make errors, or you won't get business. Not long ago I was called back to a firm for an error. O.K., they were right. It was an error—my error. It was down in black and white. I can't understand. I've done that firm's books for fifteen years. They know the caliber of my work. An audit picked up the mistake. A stupid slip. Sure they understood. It was all passed over, but I caught the president of the firm looking at me. "Tired?" he asked. "Working hard?" I could have hit him one. You know, the fact is it shows I'm not a machine—the machine I thought I was. But I can't afford this happening again. Put me on my guard. Made me edgy. I never had that feeling of wanting or needing to do a double check on my work. With me it was the first go-around that was right. You get cagey about yourself when something like this happens. If it was someone else, I'd understand. What do I do? Tell myself I'm sorry— don't let it happen again.

Problems develop, little ones, big ones, middle-sized problems—and the rise to the top no longer seems so rosy, or inevitable, or even possible. In most cases, the actual problems are no more than those he has met dozens of times in the past. But at thirty or thirty-five, he took them in his stride. They were simply part of the everyday challenge of work, and he met them with confidence and courage. But now, as he reaches for the fulfillment of his ambitions, they take on new meaning. It is no longer just a case lost, a paper rejected, a sale that wasn't successful. It becomes part of a larger pattern, the beginnings of self-doubt, the loss of confidence.

A forty-three-year-old executive in a clothing manufacturing firm had always entertained the notion of opening his
own business. Although financially able, he holds back—
hesitant about starting off on his own at his age.

I've been in the business now for twenty years. Started
on the road as a salesman. After I was married I worked
for a big firm here in the city. I've always wanted my
own place. It takes money. I didn't have that kind of
money. You get a raise and it's eaten up in taxes or the
kids need something.

I had a lucky break on the stock market a few years
ago—not a fortune, but enough to put aside for my
own business. Now when I got the capital, all I read in
the papers is how the world is falling apart. It's no time
to plunge. My wife and I talk about it. I've been working for other people all these years. Now when I want
to start out on my own there's a recession. What do you
do? Say the hell with the economy and open up a place?
Do I leave the security I have and start on my own? I've
got seniority. I can't move up and become a partner
where I'm at. It's a family-owned business, and I see
the cards on the table. The grandson will take over. I
won't be out, but I won't be in. I'll be in the same place
—a good job, steady living.

I told my wife maybe I should go ahead anyhow.
Forget the economy. We can ride along easy until
things pick up. She says no. Maybe she's right. We got
kids to think about. What if the business doesn't go
and there's a long depression? I'd be out of a job. Each
year it was going to be next year. That's O.K. when
you're thirty. You don't think about the years ahead.
Now, I'm no chicken. I'm forty-three and I got this
feeling if I don't do it now, I'll never do it. But now
I have responsibilities. Sometimes when I sit at the
desk I look out of the window. I say to myself, "You're

stuck. Face it. That's life—a place to live, food on the
table. Forget the dream. Keep the money at a safe six
percent for retirement."

In his early forties a man finds himself thinking that
maybe he won't become the next Freud or Einstein, or
president of the company—he won't write a brilliant novel,
paint a truly great picture, make a million dollars.

Typically, when the doubts begin, his initial reaction is to
increase the sheer amount of work he tries to do. But the
verve that characterized his earlier bursts of effort is gone.
There is a doggedness, a sense of grim determination. Hours
pile up, not happy hours, and not necessarily productive
hours—just hours of minutiae that leave him even more
tired, and perhaps even more self-doubting.

He no longer feels like the young man on his way up, and
he no longer looks or acts the part. In small and subtle ways,
he passes from "young man on the way up" to "senior man
holding his own." This doesn't mean that movement up the
ladder of power and position stops; by and large, it continues
as he consolidates his gains and reaps the rewards of his
earlier work, his increased skill and his experience. But the
pace of his upward momentum begins to slow down, and he
becomes more aware of the difficulties, the problems, the
increasing price that must be paid for continued advancement. As a result, from his own point of view, he becomes
more "realistic," down-to-earth, practical—and also more
responsible. He comes to appreciate the role of luck, both
good and bad, and realizes that life, unlike a 1930's movie,
doesn't always have a sweet and happy ending. Bit by bit,
the dreams and goals of earlier years become less sharp, less
compelling. With his growing self-doubt, his sense of ines-
capable responsibilities, the consciousness of his own human
weaknesses and mortality, he becomes aware of the passing
of his promise, as a forty-two-year-old chairman of a high
school English department does when he talks about stu-

dents' ambitions, his own dream, and his conviction that
when the great American novel is written, he won't be
author.

Year after year I hear the same stories from kids in my
classes. I get one who's going to write the great American novel, another who's going to be a star in the
theater, a kid who plans on a Nobel Prize in science.
Dreams you hear in conferences. What do you tell
them? Pack the dreams up and file them away and plan
on a safe job, maybe one with tenure like I have in a
good suburban high school? I wonder.
  I've enjoyed my teaching. I won't deny that. And
I've been a damn good teacher. But I'm not kidding
myself about my own ambitions. Twenty years ago
when I took my first teaching job that wasn't what I
wanted. Teaching gave me freedom—summers free,
time off, good hours, O.K. pay—enough to live on—
but I planned on a writing career. I was going to teach
for a few years, then write a novel, get a job on a
magazine—move up beyond to the big time. And instead I settled for what I got, and somewhere between
then and now are years I can't separate in my mind.
  I ran into an old high school buddy. He's a lawyer
—was going to be a big-shot judge. He had got hooked
on Clarence Darrow when we were in high school. Was
even going to change his name. He's got an office now
—second floor in a two-story brick building with a pizza
parlor on the first. He makes good money, thanks to
divorce rates going up, as he put it. There isn't one
damn thing wrong with our lives. We have healthy
kids, nice homes. So what's the big deal? He's not
Clarence Darrow, and I'm not Ernest Hemmingway.
Then what gives? I don't know myself, except you
wonder could you have done anything to make it end
just a bit differently. Like me. Did I make the try? Did

I give up before I started? Maybe that's the book to write—the story of a talented kid who, at forty-two, says to himself, "Now or never," and he knows damn well it's never.

The Threat of Impotence

"What really bothered him was sex."

In his early forties a man is likely to be working longer hours than ever before. Suspecting that he may not reach the pinnacle of success he had hoped for, he becomes concerned about missing the next big chance, and worried about setbacks that once seemed trivial. He feels the tension of possible failure, the fear of being overlooked, passed over, of losing a crucial opportunity. He becomes especially sensitive to any sign that others may be losing confidence in him. Minor aches and ills are no longer viewed as minor; major illness no longer seems impossible. Fatigue, tension, worry, stress and strain gradually build—and it is not at all remarkable that his sex life—like that of this forty-three-year-old owner of a restaurant—becomes less active. His wife describes the problems they have had recently in their sexual relationship.

Lately he's been getting home later and later. He usually is very tired, and after dinner and perhaps the late news we go to bed. And I mean that quite literally. We go to bed. He goes to sleep the minute his head touches the pillow. Of course I'm bothered. I haven't said anything because of what happened the last time we tried to have intercourse. It was quite disturbing for him. He couldn't perform. And he became angry. He didn't say anything. I told him maybe he was tired from over-working.

That only got him angrier. It was embarrassing for him. I knew that. What could I say? He got out of bed, and went into the bathroom and took a shower. He exploded again because the kids had used up all the shampoo, and he wanted to wash his hair. I said I forgot to buy shampoo, and he said what the hell did I do all day. The least I could do was to remember to buy shampoo.

What really bothered him was sex. I told him so, and he said I was hardly the most attractive person physi-cally and why the hell I didn't do something about my hair. It just started to build up about petty things, and I thought we would wake the kids, so I went downstairs and had coffee, and just sat until I was sure he was asleep.

He left early in the morning without having break-fast. I tried calling him at the restaurant. The cashier told me he wasn't around, and I said to forget it be-cause it wasn't important. He came in that evening and was pleasant—so was I. We didn't mention the subject. I think it will just take a while until he's less tense. I thought I should wait before talking about the problem again; and sex will just have to wait. I thought maybe I should get a fancy nightgown—seriously. I'm not a candidate for a Playboy photograph, but then neither is he a pinup picture. I'm not angry at him. I don't blame him; but I don't want to feel it's all my fault.

Perhaps for the first time in his life he finds it difficult to achieve and maintain an erection, and no amount of fore-play will do the job. If he does manage an erection, reaching orgasm may be a dreary and tension-producing business, with little zest and still less pleasure.

It is unlikely that he views his decreased sexual drive as a natural consequence of emotional strain and physical fatigue. He is more likely to experience it as the first sign of the dreaded loss of potency, of masculinity. The more he worries about it, of course, the greater the difficulty he encounters. The failure of his penis to become readily erect, and to remain firmly so, takes on an overload of psychological meaning that is resonant with stresses from other areas of his life. It is a serious threat to his sense of competence and power.

The wife of a forty-three-year-old internist with an extensive private practice expressed concern about a significant change in her husband's sexual patterns.

I've been quite troubled about his behavior. It's not that we're fighting or not getting along, but we haven't had sexual relations in months. I find it terribly hard to understand. There isn't anyone else. I'm sure of that. He's not the kind to run around—stay out late, take weekends away. I'm no fool. I would know if there's someone else he's seeing. He just can't have an erection. We've tried and that's it. He just can't. He gets out of bed and is upset. Goes down and has something to drink. I hate facing him knowing how he must feel. It's making him very tense. He paces the floor. I hear him. And he doesn't fall off to sleep easily. He keeps turning over, pounding his pillow into shapes. We've kept trying. Nothing like this has ever happened before. If anything, I've been the one to be mechanical sometimes, but that's because I was tired or the kids wore me out—but never him. If anything, he could be at me four times a day. He'd even kid about his power —sort of a standing joke—equal to four males and he was going to up the score. Well, that has changed. I wonder if he worries about it. I certainly do.

It is extremely difficult for him to accept these sexual difficulties as his own fault—a reflection of his loss of potency. Instead of blaming himself, he can much more comfortably conclude that it is his wife's fault—it is *she* who is no longer sexually attractive, not he who is losing his sexual potency. He protects his battered ego by simply switching the source of the trouble. In this way he may come to believe that he has trouble achieving and maintaining an erection because there is nothing in his bed worthy of an erection. Indeed, his wife may have gained a few pounds and lost the sleek looks of her youth. She may no longer devote herself to the sometimes arduous task of appearing to be, and being, seductive. She may wear a flannel nightgown to keep warm rather than a satin negligee to generate sexual heat. And from his point of view, sex with her involves the same old routine performance, repeated hundreds of times in the past —*sans* surprise, *sans* mystery, *sans* excitement.

Thus, his stubbornly flaccid penis is her fault, her responsibility, her failure—and it becomes a central piece of evidence in his heightening concern about whether or not his marriage was right in the first place.

The Family Rut

"Why am I going to bed and getting up day after day with the same person?"

An important aspect of a man's identity over the years has derived from his roles in marriage and the family. Thus, as part of the more general crisis in which he questions his own identity, he begins to brood—like this forty-two-year-old manager of a shoe store—about his role as husband and father. Faced with the sexual freedoms of today's adolescents, he questions his value system and his wife's moral code.

My wife is hung up on the new youth morality—you know, kids trying it out, living together, before deciding whether or not they want to get married. My nephew just broke up with some girl he had been living with. Three years and now he tells his parents they weren't suited for each other. Maybe the kids today are smarter than we were. They give themselves a chance to find out what it's like going to bed and getting up day after day with the same person.

In my time we had only Saturday nights to find out what the other person was like. It was an act for both of us—a front. We weren't ourselves. And we kept up Saturday nights until we got married. You know something—the novelty with each other probably would have worn off quickly with a few straight weekends in bed, but that wasn't the style.

We had our hangups. Then after it's legal you learn to make do, struggle along making the best of the deal. After a while you realize that Saturday nights didn't tell you the whole story. I've got a great wife, but after the first few years there were differences I never realized before we were married—differences that don't get any smaller as time goes on. Who knows? Maybe if I had had more time she would have been the one I would have chosen anyhow; but I don't know—I never gave myself the chance to find out. That's why if kids today want to try living together it's fine with me. It's easier to get out of a relationship before you get tied up in legal knots.

"Was my marriage the right one? Has it been a mistake?"
These doubts are reenforced by his boredom with the everyday routines of family life and his bridling resentment of
responsibilities that have accumulated over the years. A
leaky faucet needs to be repaired; someone has to take the
car to the garage for an oil change; the checkbook is out of
whack again and must be balanced; the family must pay its
annual visit to boring relatives; friends are coming to dinner
Friday for another dull evening because "we owe them";
someone has to talk to the children about getting homework
done, and someone has to lay down the law about coming
home on time; the bathroom needs painting, the dentist
needs paying, cousins need calling—"My God! Is this what
life is all about? Does marriage have to mean leaky faucets,
whining kids, boring relatives?"

For the most part, his reactions are largely gloomy grum-
blings of doubt. But there is another aspect of emotional
expression that comes to play an increasingly important part
in marriage. Society recognizes marriage as a major institution for the legitimate satisfaction of sexual needs. But marriage is also the "safest" relationship in which to satisfy the
need to express aggression. The man in his early forties
cannot readily blow up at work or with his friends because
of the social restraints he has learned and the real danger of
counter-aggression from the outside world. But within the
confines of marriage and the family, these inhibitions can be
dropped from time to time, the controls on behavior somewhat relaxed; it is simply safer to explode at home.

A sixteen-year-old girl vividly described her maneuvers
with her forty-three-year-old father to avoid his outbursts of
temper.

If I wait until the right time I can get anything I want
from my Dad. I don't ask a lot, really. I mean, maybe
money for a new sweater or skirt or just anything I
want. I've gotten to where I can read him like a book.
If he comes home and the first thing he says is "Who

in the hell left skates in the middle of the garage?" I beat it. I told my mom she isn't as good as I am. She'll go on in her own way or answer him back. I shut up. That's what I mean about reading his moods.

But other times he's great. I think he's better than all the fathers of my friends. My girl friend's father never says a word when he comes home, and half the time he works late. My dad tries, though. He works hard, and last week he asked me why the two of us didn't go out more together. He's taking me out Saturday afternoon, and he said we could go anywhere I want to. He does things like this, and I know he cares about me. He always wants to know what I'm doing in school. I shouldn't complain about him, but there are some bad times too—he just explodes and bangs the dishes and acts terrible to Mom. I can't understand. It just comes on, and no one has done anything, but he is yelling and banging doors and blaming everyone in the house. I just want to run away when he gets started. I get all tight inside, and I maybe go outside and sit just anywhere where I can't hear his voice.

Temper tantrums don't occur only during the early forties, but they do have special meaning at this time, for this is a period of life when frustration becomes almost a daily experience. As a result of this frustration, a good deal of aggression is generated, aggression which cannot easily be expressed in the outside world, particularly when that world is already perceived as threatening. It is not at all surprising that the aggression generated by the frustrations of work during this period, doubts about himself, his questions about his own identity as husband and father, are expressed by stormy explosions in the family, bitter complaints about the stifling routines and responsibilities he feels imposed upon him by his wife and children.

The wife of a forty-three-year-old pharmacist who owns

his own drugstore felt confused and upset by her husband's tantrums, which seemed to occur over trivial matters.

Lately I don't know what's got into him. He flies off the handle if you look at him wrong. Well, not all the time. But his temper about little things has me terribly confused. There are times he's a real angel, and other times I could lose my mind. The other morning is a good example. I had gone to the bakery early and brought home Danish for breakfast. It was Sunday—I remember, because we get up late on Sundays. He came downstairs, and I had the Danish and coffee on the table— cream cheese, butter. It couldn't have been nicer. He sat down, took a Danish, and then slammed it on the plate. It was awful. He started to yell at me about why in the hell I bought Danish with raisins when I know that he hates raisins in his Danish and has hated them for twenty-two years.

I told him I didn't know there were raisins in the Danish. Are you blind? he shouted. He picked up a Danish and pushed it in front of my face. He asked me what in the hell were those brown things if they weren't raisins. I told him at the time in the bakery I hadn't realized there were raisins. Maybe the others didn't have raisins. They all have raisins, he told me. He said I never learned, that I was just being my usual inconsiderate self.

The fact is the bakery was crowded. It really slipped my mind. He said that it wasn't so, and that I had done it purposefully. Imagine all this about raisins in a Danish. He wouldn't have breakfast and went back upstairs. I felt terrible. The whole morning was ruined. A scene over raisins. I could understand if it were something major in our lives. But to have him fighting, screaming, breaking dishes about raisins upset me. I don't understand what is happening to him. He never behaved like that in all the years I can remember—not about something like raisins in Danish, that's for sure.

Although doubt and aggression are central issues in family relationships at this time, other changes in behavior reflect the complexity of this developmental crisis. These other changes, in fact, seem to contradict the hostile tone of his outbursts of temper and his brooding rejection of those close to him. For example, in the demanding days of his middle and late thirties, he may have acquired a relatively hard-driving style in his work. He was primarily concerned with establishing his position and moving up the ladder of economic success. He had to work hard, he had to push himself and others, and to some extent this quality was bound to spill over into his family relationships. Thus, his wife and children might have seen him as somewhat brittle, perhaps too demanding, and unconcerned with or unaware of the more subtle nuances of interpersonal relations within the family.

But with the developmental crisis of the early forties, this brittle, hard-driving quality often becomes less apparent in family relationships. There may be an increased tenderness, a greater concern with those who are close to him, a gentler tone that softens day-to-day interactions. At one moment, he may be explosively angry, hostile, critical; a short time later, he may be unusually thoughtful, kind, and sensitive. At one time he may be withdrawn, seemingly unreachable; later on, he may become warm and friendly, lively and full of fun. The emotional tone is inconsistent, changing without apparent external causes. Both anger and affection, withdrawal and concern characterize his behavior—reflecting internal conflicts about his identity as both husband and father.

In the late thirties a man's emotional life is characterized by a sense of excitement, vitality, challenge, and adventure. This general tone is carried over as the decade of the forties commences, but with the onset of his developmental crisis, he begins to brood—about himself, the world, death, "the meaning of it all." He frequently feels sorry for himself, alternating between feeling "the world is no damned good" and his fearful suspicion that *"I* am fundamentally no good." He has bouts of delicious melancholy, delicious because he tends to romanticize his feelings. This melancholy reflects his concern with the larger issues of life. He develops a sense of being a person above and beyond the mundane and trivial, and from time to time, with a gentle sigh, he senses that in his melancholy he has somehow tasted the bittersweet core of human existence.

This brooding is punctuated by hostile explosions that leave him feeling guilty and tired. His emotional life is further complicated by events that confront him with the fact of his own mortality, so there are moments of dread that reenforce his enveloping moodiness.

A manager of a hardware store and lumberyard reported his sense of being overwhelmed by the complexities of living. Forty-three years of age, he reminisced about a time in his life when he felt carefree.

After forty maybe more happens to you or maybe you're just aware of problems. All I know is that I get this feeling of knots around me. Sure there are plenty of times I feel on top of the world, but lately more and more the knots. I suppose I'm just realizing I'm not free like I was at twenty-two. I'm settled down—I remember the time when everything I owned could fit in the back trunk of a car I had—a small car. Now the trunk won't even hold the kids' winter clothes. You know, boots, shoes, gloves, hats—I don't know half the junk they have. Not one car—two cars—a house, bills, a whole world of first-of-the-month checks to write, and another month, and that's the way the years stretch out. It's like you had a short breath of freedom and then somebody puts you in a compression chamber and they keep turning knobs. I got so many people dependent on me now—my folks getting older, the kids, wife, and why in the hell we added a dog and a canary. I feel some days I could strangle the canary, as if it's that bird's fault I've got all this on my shoulders, when, like I told you, there was a time when everything I owned could fit in the small trunk of a little car I had—a secondhand car with 50,000 miles on it. I drove it for another fifty thousand before it landed in the junkyard.

middle forties

Explosions

"I've got to cut loose."

The man experiencing the crisis of the early forties feels trapped in his distress. But it is precisely this distress that can lead to a resolution of the crisis and the possibility of growth. By and large, the changes in behavior that mark significant steps in psychological development do not stem from feelings of ease and contentment. When one is satisfied with his life and himself, his everyday behavior tends to remain relatively stable. Comfort breeds a kind of psychological inertia; one does today what one did the day before —and the day before that. This pattern of inertia, however, is disrupted by the challenges that confront the man in his early forties, the threats to his sense of identity as husband and father, as a productive, achieving, virile adult. The beliefs of his earlier life no longer seem so obviously valid or self-evident. He is jolted from the rut of his existence, and with the jolt comes a chance for change.

A forty-seven-year-old senior computer programmer reflected on the creeping monotony of his life. He perceived his present life-style as a one-way trip on a dead-end street.

I was driving to work. Usually I listen to the radio— takes my mind off traffic. I don't think; I listen. But the radio wouldn't work that morning. The aerial was ripped off when I left the car parked on the street. I sat in traffic for two hours. A trailer truck had a flat, and

cars were backed up for miles. You sit like I did in a
stalled car, staring at cars in front of you, inhaling
monoxide from exhausts, and you say to yourself,
"What the hell am I doing? This is my life?" For
twenty-three years, since I finished grad school, I've
been making the same trip—it's insanity. I can't take
it. Locked in a car stuck on a highway.

I get to an office building, and I go up an elevator,
and I get locked up the rest of the day. Not one thing
about that damn office interests me any more. Sure I
used to have fun and look at programs as challenges. I
think I kidded myself. Now I tell you every step I make
to that office is a drag. Programs bore the hell out of
me. I've dealt with the same problems over and over.
You know I could fill in programs before someone tells
me what he needs. They're all the same. All those years
I worked—what do they add up to? It took a broken
radio in the car to make me think—to make me wake
up to the monotony of my life. I'm being choked to
death. I've got to cut loose. I don't want to be locked
up. I don't want the routine. I don't want to get up
every morning, get in traffic lines, inch the car along a
road that only leads to a dead-end.

At forty-six, the regional manager for a large food corporation sensed a loss of direction in himself. A disturbing dream
triggered self-doubt.

I had this dream—only once—but it stays in my mind.
My father called me on the telephone. He was lost.
Asked me for directions. Said he couldn't find my
house. Told me where he was. It was only a few blocks
from where I lived. I told him how to get to my place.
Keep walking two blocks, turn, another block. The
connection was bad and I wasn't sure he heard me. I

woke up at that point. My father has been dead for
eight years.
  You know the next days I kept asking myself, "What
did the dream mean?" He lost? Maybe it was me.
Maybe I'm sick of being the one holding the bag. The
kids turn to me. My wife turns to me. The office turns
to me. I don't know, but it disturbed me. Look, don't
get me wrong. If you added up my balance sheet, I got
a lot going for me. Then why this feeling of being lost?
My dad lost—or was it me? I'm the one dead inside.
That dream was damned real. I tell you, the next morning when I woke up, I swear I felt the telephone in my
hand.

There begins a period of rapidly changing behavior, motivated by the discomfort of crisis and the search for a resolution. There is a flurry of new ideas, tastes, values, goals.
Some are fleeting, lasting an hour, a day, a week; others seem
to gain greater import and stability—and then disappear as
new changes continue to occur. It is an unstable period, and
sometimes the behavior seems to represent an almost random search for novelty. But in fact, the behavior is neither
random nor entirely novel, for it inevitably reflects the conflicts, wishes, dreams, and defenses of the past. Thus, a new
stage appears within the overall pattern of this decade, the
middle forties—a time of trial and a time of error.
  A man in his middle forties is sometimes accused of
returning to childhood, and indeed some of his behavior
may appear to be childish, or perhaps more accurately,
"adolescentish." However, this does not represent a psychological regression in the technical sense of a return to an
earlier stage of development. Rather, these are short-term
regressions that are part of the process of experimentation,
trial, and error. He is appropriately concerned with testing
and trying out new behaviors, attitudes, ideologies. The

structure of his former identity has been shaken by the trauma of the early forties, and quite reasonably, he is striving to forge an identity that will provide a firmer basis for his life.

These changes in behavior are therefore not childish or neurotic; they are healthy reactions to stress. As a matter of fact, one might realistically be more concerned about the person who does not respond actively to the crisis of the early forties—the man who withdraws into depression, living a half-life. In a very real sense, he has committed a form of psychological suicide. There is no doubt that his inconsistent, occasionally extreme, and seemingly immature behavior patterns cause considerable difficulty in his own life and in the lives of those who are close to him. Nevertheless, it is far better for him to respond actively and energetically to the crisis of this decade than to passively retreat into despair.

If his behavior appears to be adolescent-like, it is partly because the nature of the crisis he faces is in some ways similar to the crisis faced by the adolescent. Nevertheless, there are significant differences that derive from the fact that he has a history that the adolescent does not have. He has lived in certain roles for over twenty years, and has an investment in continuing in them. He has acquired some skills, status, power, and prerogatives, as well as responsibilities to others. Therefore, the experimentation, the trials and errors necessary for psychological growth in the middle forties are, in some respects, more stressful and demanding than the parallel experience in adolescence. This man is not engaged in forming a new identity, but in recasting and reshaping an already established one, he must break down some of the structures of the past. He must give up well-learned habits. He must relinquish old perspectives while at the same time searching for newer points of view. Thus, he experiences the stress of both breaking with his past and building for his future.

Moreover, he is engaged in this complex process of

growth within a context of day-to-day responsibilities from which he cannot easily escape. During the trials of a teenage identity crisis, the adolescent need not worry about bills to be paid, a family to be cared for, a business to run. He can safely withdraw into an egocentric world, protected from the harsher realities of life. But the middle-forties man cannot afford this luxury. He must deal with these external realities while struggling with his internal conflicts. He cannot take "time out," a moratorium; he is like this forty-seven-year-old advertising executive reacting to the constant pressures of his job, friends, and family.

I thought I could take it. The rat race was nothing for me when I first started this game. It's not the same. I'm feeling I've had it. The calls start in the morning even before I leave the house. Then my kids and my wife. They act like I got nothing on my mind but their problems. It's go, go, go, constantly. I tell you, I'd give anything for a few hours to myself, time to think about myself. I'm sick of being on the giving end. I get this feeling sometimes I got to escape. I'd like to dump the whole business—job, family, people, everything—but you can't. You got to wade through it, and you got to stick it out. When I get ten minutes I lock myself in the men's room at the office and sit there and meditate. It's the only time I really get for myself.

There is little wonder that the behavior of the man in his middle forties may sometimes appear to be irrational, inappropriate, immature. But he is not behaving childishly out of some whim or innate wickedness. Nor is he merely selfish or silly. His sometimes astonishing variety of behaviors is part of an overall pattern of personal development. It is a period of great promise, a time when major strides can be taken in the direction of greater autonomy and self-realization. In this sense, it is indeed a childlike stage of life, for it is only in childhood that we find a similar potential for leaps in maturity within a brief span of time. Thus, if we view life in the mid-forties as like that of a child, it is in the positive sense of being in a process of dynamic growth and fulfillment.

The Conjugal Battleground

"She doesn't understand me."

For many years, the roles of husband and father have been central components of the identity of the man in his middle forties. He has defined himself, in part, through his relationships with his wife and children, and over the years of his marriage, these relationships have required a substantial psychic investment. When he thinks about the kind of person he is, he may consider a wide variety of traits and behaviors, goals and beliefs. But regardless of the other ways in which he thinks about himself, his characteristics as husband and father almost always play a major part in his sense of personal identity. It is not at all surprising, therefore, that these aspects of his life become important battlegrounds on which he fights the war of his identity.

Perhaps his most common marital complaint is boredom. There's nothing new any more; they've said the same words, done the same things a hundred times before. There are no surprises, no discoveries; the excitement is gone.

He asks himself, "How did I ever get caught in this trap?" He may recall the eager anticipation before they were married, the fun of their first few years, the challenges of having children. Then, without knowing why or when or how it changed, it all seems different—dull and flat. It's as if he turned his back for a moment, and when he turned around again, all the joy and liveliness were gone. All that's left are petty and boring responsibilities. Marriage is a trap—not painful, just boring—and he feels hemmed in, blocked and frustrated.

There is, of course, some basis in external reality for these complaints. Family life—everyone's life—would be impossible without a certain degree of order, some routine. Having lived together for fifteen or twenty years, a man and his wife are hardly strangers to each other, and at a superficial level at least, there are undoubtedly fewer surprises, fewer opportunities for fresh discoveries. By this time the novelty has surely worn off, and the excitement of living with an almost-stranger is a thing of the past. There is, in fact, the same demanding and familiar regularity in his marital life that a real estate developer, who had just celebrated a forty-seventh birthday, describes.

> Don't let anyone kid you. Marriage is a rut. Sure you start off with ideas—it's going to be different, exciting. So you have a few years and then you settle back and it's the same thing day in and day out. No change—no life—just the same thing day after day. I told my wife, "Look at me—I get new ideas, new interests." What the hell is life about? She's happy vegetating, sitting back. Likes the same things. I tell her, "Come on, let's do something different." No, she's got to plan, so we forget about it. For her life is a routine to live through. For me the house, the kids, the lists she makes up of things to do are a bore. I've been through it day after day, year after year.

Complaints of boredom in his marriage are to some extent a projection of his boredom with himself. He achieved his basic identity as an adult over twenty years ago, and since that time he has been *himself*—more or less thinking the same kinds of thoughts, doing the same kinds of things, feeling the same kinds of feelings. He has undoubtedly changed somewhat, grown older, more mature, but his ways of thinking, doing, and feeling have remained relatively constant, and if he experiences a certain "sameness" about his life, it is rooted in his own identity.

Moreover, that identity is being challenged, and he reacts to the threat with anxiety and hostility thinly disguised as boredom with his marriage. When he says, "I am bored with my wife," he means "I am anxious and angry, and I blame my wife." He is responding to stress in a very human way —projecting the blame onto others and indirectly expressing aggression. After all, to say "I am bored in your company" is not quite as obvious as saying "I am angry with you," but it carries the same essentially aggressive meaning. It is a civilized, semi-polite form of attack.

Marital attacks of the mid-forties man, however, are not always so indirect or even semi-polite. Sometimes his aggression is blatant and direct. For example, there is often during this period a marked upsurge in the force and frequency with which he criticizes his wife. Thus, family disagreements may erupt into full-scale battles.

Whatever the substantive content of the attack might be, it often reflects his concerns about himself, though at the time of his attack, he may not be consciously aware of this self-concern. If he has been feeling a bit potty, hefty around the hips, sluggish and slow, it is not at all unlikely that he will explode at his wife, accusing her of failing to remain sleek and slim. If he is feeling intellectually tired and dulled in the heat of a family argument, he may very well announce to his wife that she just doesn't know what she is talking about.

A husband's criticism of his wife is not unique to this period of married life. However, the emotional strength of these critical comments does show a sharp rise during this stage. Naturally his wife is sometimes confused and overwhelmed by these outbursts. True enough, she might have gained some weight. But in the easier days before the time of crisis, she and her husband might have talked about her weight, joked about it, and he might have reassured her that she actually looked better than ever. But now, the few pounds may become a monumental issue, and her husband no longer is supportively reassuring.

Of course, the focus of attack might not be weight. It might just as well be her cooking, her housekeeping, her clothes, her manners, her make-up, her child-rearing, her lack of knowledge—in short, anything that happens to reverberate with her husband's own self-concerns.

The wife of an executive in his middle forties talked about her husband's incessant critical evaluation of everything about her.

If you asked him to describe me, he'd probably tell you I'm an ignorant mess. I don't know what has gotten into him. He's started at me about my hair, figure, personality. For twenty-four years I haven't been a wreck. Suddenly I'm a terrible person. He says he's always felt that way. I just can't believe him. I'm not that bad. I have a very nice figure for my age. It isn't easy. I fight every pound. I can't remember the last time I had butter. A slice of bread to me is like an ice cream to a kid. What more can I do? I get my hair done. From my point of view I'm an intelligent, attractive woman in her forties. No, I'm not twenty. No, I can't play thirty-six holes of golf in the morning and another round in the afternoon. I can't take up water skiing, get all that excited about politics. But then there are things I like to do that he doesn't. Has he read some of the books I've been reading? Has he bothered to take off the weight he's gained? I wouldn't dare tell him.

He'd explode and accuse me of being defensive, not facing myself, trying to shift the blame onto him. It's a difficult time for me. I've got to do all the changing. And I'm concerned. I can't be a pinup girl, a prime minister, an athletic star, gourmet chef, and a high-priced prostitute all in one day.

For his part, the husband may even realize that he has become more critical, and may even be aware of the emotional force of his reactions. But rarely does he see that these responses derive mainly from his own concerns about himself. More often, he rationalizes his behavior with statements such as "It's better to be honest." He mumbles that he has known her shortcomings for a long time, but he has controlled himself, tried to protect her from reality.

These are not just excuses made to explain his behavior to others. He really believes them, especially right after a battle. He convinces himself, and earnestly tries to convince his wife, that the criticisms he offers are made in good faith, and always in her own best interests. After all, who should know better her faults than he who has "suffered" all these years? Though it be painful for both of them, it is time for the truth to be spoken, and occasionally also shouted.

A financial executive in his mid-forties talked about his efforts to help his wife change.

I tell her over and over she has to face up to what she's become. She hides behind a mask. For years I've kept quiet, not said a word to her about the way she keeps herself, the house, her behavior with my friends. O.K., it's time she takes a good square look at herself. You don't find me staying the same. I told her this. Now she has to get with it. She's lagging behind and not going to catch up. There's a world out there, and she isn't any different from the day I married her. She tells me she has changed. "How?" I ask her. She'll never change.

She's shut out everything that doesn't suit her. We got to have everything in the house the way it was when we moved in. We got to do the same things, see the same people, sex in the same way. That's what I mean, she's got her feet in cement. I can't get her moving along. And to be frank I'm not terribly interested in trying any more.

Stunned and hurt, his wife may at first retreat, not infrequently in tears. But then, psychologically battered and bruised, she may begin to counterattack. If she has gained a few pounds, she can also point to the increasing size of his waist. If she has failed to keep up with her husband's interests, how much does he know about her activities? If he is bored with her, how does he think she feels about him, his brooding and his complaints?

Thus, the battle is joined. Among some couples, the battles are fought openly, with emotional fireworks. Among others, the battles are largely underground, somewhat quieter but just as hostile. Regardless of the volume of noise, there is mutual suffering.

A sales engineer nearing a forty-sixth birthday noted that marital battles drained him psychologically.

Maybe she thinks I'm happy about the bickering. It starts in the morning. Anything can set it off. I'm not the one at fault. Today I asked her was there any orange juice. I didn't accuse her, but she got hurt. Well, the fact is she should have remembered to get orange juice. I certainly do my share of the work around the house. She can carry her weight. From orange juice we can go right on, and by the time I leave for work my stomach is in knots. I could explode. I am depressed the whole day. I feel like hell. The whole world is sour. I don't want to face people. I want to get away. It's a terrible way to live. When I turn my key in the door at night,

I stand there and think about the explosions we have. I feel rotten. She tells me she's the one suffering because of my temper. It's unbelievable to me. She doesn't even see that I am suffering inside. I'm in real pain. I'm suffering a helluva lot more than she ever could for what's happening between us.

Although the middle-forties husband may be the more overt and seemingly stronger aggressor in these marital battles, he is in fact unusually vulnerable. His own hostile behavior stems primarily from the identity crisis in which he finds himself. More than at any other time in his adult life, he is insecure. Therefore, when his wife begins to counterattack, he is quite likely to be seriously hurt. Thus, though he frequently initiates the marital battle, in the course of the fight, it is often he who is hurt more.

From these intense, usually irrational, and almost always painful battles there develops a theme that becomes increasingly powerful in the husband's experience of his marriage. Perhaps this theme can best be summarized by the phrase "She doesn't understand me."

A forty-five-year-old buyer for a clothing chain feels his wife hasn't developed over the years. Currently involved with encounter therapy groups, he's become aware of the lack of real feeling in his marital relationship.

My wife hasn't changed since when we were first married. You know, when you're twenty-five you need someone who is a lot of fun. My wife was a lot of fun —a good sport. Lots of guys were after her. But she has stayed twenty-five emotionally. She hasn't developed new interests that count. She's fine when it come to the superficialities of life. She reads, likes music, theater, takes courses at a university, but where it really counts —basic understanding of me as a person—she misses the mark completely. I'm not talking about intellectual exchanges. I'm talking about real feeling, knowing what it is that makes me a real person—that's where she draws a blank.

I can't talk to her any more. She wouldn't understand. I'm a very sensitive person. She sees me differently. She sees me like I was twenty-five, thirty; hasn't any awareness of how much I've changed. She puts up a wall. Every time I try and talk to her, sit down and really get at real feelings she finds something to do or switches the subject. She hasn't any understanding of my emotional life. I go to these group therapy sessions —I don't need therapy, but a friend had me come to some open encounter groups. I find them interesting. Other guys, I'm finding out, are having the same problems. I wonder if it has something to do with our society—you get married to one woman, and you let the marriage drag on for years and years without thinking of what really happens. I don't blame my wife. I don't blame myself. The simple fact is I've changed— I'm very sensitive—she wasn't when I married her, and she certainly hasn't developed.

And of course, in a sense, he is right. Most wives confronted by middle-forties behavior in their husbands *don't* understand what is going on, and they may feel that a nightmare has somehow intruded into their previously peaceful and pleasant lives. However, the fact that his wife doesn't fully comprehend the complex dynamics of his current life does not entirely account for his repeated complaint. There is another dimension to this theme that stems from his own psychological confusion. The complaint is also an indication of his lack of self-understanding. Thus, he projects his own confusion onto his wife, and instead of saying "I don't understand myself," he can more comfortably say and believe "My wife doesn't understand me." In addition, of course, this phrase can serve as a ready rationalization to cover a wide range of extramarital activities that he might otherwise find it difficult to excuse.

Up to this point we have focused primarily on the more hostile dynamics of the middle-forties husband. However, there is another, more positive, and in the long run, more important aspect of his marital behavior. This involves his experimentation with a variety of marital roles, his trial-and-error search for a redefinition of himself as husband.

The wife of a forty-six-year-old jewelry-store owner noted the inconsistencies of her husband's behavior.

One minute he's a doll, and the next minute I could lose my mind. He's worse than one of the kids. I shouldn't complain. Last week he walks in with a present for me. "What gives?" I say to him. It's not our anniversary—which he never remembers anyhow—or my birthday. So what's going on? He gets angry. Tells me he brings home a present for me, and I give him the third-degree like I was suspicious. "I'm not suspicious," I told him, but what do you expect I should think—a present without an occasion. I told him the last time I remember him buying a present for me without an excuse, like a birthday, was once before we were married. He told me O.K., he wouldn't do it again.

Honestly, I didn't want to hurt his feelings. I was very pleased. I told him so. But between you and me, I wouldn't be caught dead wearing a black lace nightgown. Luckily, the salesgirl had left the receipt in the box, and I could exchange it for a pants suit I really wanted. His intentions were good, but what taste! That's what I mean—a doll one day, and the next, a scene over nothing—nothing at all.

At times, he may be coy, charming, flattering, teasing, flirtatious—and when his wife fails to respond in a similar vein, he is likely to become sullen or explosively angry. At other times he shifts to the role of the totally involved family man, concerned with all the details of their home life.

The wife of a forty-six-year-old accountant talked about her husband's attempt to redecorate their living room.

He tells me, don't waste money hiring a painter. He'll do it. What's there to painting? You get paint, a brush, and you put paint on the walls. It's simple. It's been a heartache. Three walls some kind of gray and the other blue. He ran out of paint and couldn't match colors. I wanted off-white walls. It's terrible. The drapes, the furniture—nothing looks right. Then he moved the couch over to the other side of the room. I said move it back, I don't like it there. But he said change is good, and I wasn't to touch the couch. I found out why he wanted the couch over on the other side. He spilled paint. It had gone through the newspapers and made a huge spot on the carpet. Let me tell you, paint remover doesn't take paint off carpets. That's how it is —I have to live with it. The living room was something I worked hard trying to fix up. The worst is not the paint, the carpet, but him. He's blind, telling people he painted the living room and saved us money. He's proud of himself. The other day he said to me, "O.K., what next?" He's ready to start the bedrooms. I can see it happening—him destroying each room in the house one by one.

Inconsistency is the keynote of his marital behavior. Boy friend, lover, patriarch, plumber, economist, efficiency expert—he shifts from role to role in seemingly unpredictable order. This apparent inconsistency, however, is part of a larger pattern in his life at this time, and within this larger pattern the shifts from one kind of behavior to another *are* consistent and make excellent psychological sense. They represent, of course, his search for a redefined identity, a new sense of himself as husband that will be more satisfying, more appropriate and congruent with the changing circumstances and developing needs in his life. He certainly isn't easy to live with; most of his trials are fraught with errors. He doesn't consciously set out to make a fool of himself or make life inconvenient for others, though these may be the results of some of his efforts. He is not playing games or acting out make-believe roles. When he becomes the romantic suitor to the woman who has been his wife for the past ten or fifteen years, he honestly feels the romanticism of the moment. True enough, an hour before he may have been screaming about some absurdly trivial issue; and a short time later, when the romantic impulse passes, he may shift to the role of puritanical patriarch. But at the moment of his impulse, he is earnest and sincere.

His wife sometimes finds it hard to keep up with his changing behavior, let alone respond appropriately to the mood of the moment. It's like riding a roller-coaster of interpersonal relations, with dips and swirls, switchbacks and terrifying dives. At the very least, his inconsistent behavior enlivens family life, though in most instances it does much more than that. It can provoke a good deal of bickering and misunderstanding, and from time to time create havoc in the household.

During the crisis of the early forties, marital sexual activity often shows a dramatic decrease in frequency and intensity. However, as the stage of trial and error develops for the mid-forties man, there is a marked change in his sexual behavior. Like his behavior in other areas of life, the change is inconsistent, ranging from extraordinary activity to monklike abstinence. For his wife, both extremes can be nerve-racking.

A forty-seven-year-old building contractor voiced concern about his sexual activity.

I blame my wife. She doesn't do anything to make herself attractive. And the family—if all of them didn't need so damn much I wouldn't have to be killing myself to make money to support them. Sure I'm tired—damn tired at night. I got myself going and coming. It's not me, that's for sure. There's nothing wrong with me. It's what's been happening in my life. It bothers me. My wife looks at me now like something is wrong with me. The last time was pretty bad. I couldn't get it up —made me feel like a damn fool. It's not pleasant for me. I've begun thinking a lot about the problem lately. I tell myself forget it, and then I can't—slips into my mind. That kind of problem can really drive you up a wall.

Concern about virility was a central issue in the crisis he faced in his early forties. This concern continues through the next stage of development, varying both in intensity and associated behaviors. For the man in his mid-forties, worry about virility may become so strong that his sexual drive seems to disappear entirely. The more he worries about his sexual life, the worse it becomes, and no amount of seductiveness or sexual play can shake him out of his asexual shell. He may try to arouse himself via fantasies, movies, manuals on sexual techniques. Nothing seems to work. He remains sexually flat, dull, and anxious.

At other times, probably when he is less concerned about his virility, his sexual life becomes remarkably vigorous. He feels intense excitement, and his impulses may take a variety of directions—oral, anal, in various positions and settings. In Freudian terms, he seems to plunge temporarily into a state of "polymorphous perverse sexuality."

But of course it is neither perverse nor perverted; he is simply responding to a major crisis in his life by breaking out of established patterns. He is actively searching for new dimensions of an identity that will be more congruent with the conditions of his current life. As a major aspect of his identity, sexuality is bound to be a principal area of experimentation, trial and error. Thus, his bouts of heightened sexual activity and the diversity of his desires are not pathological or amoral. They are an intrinsic part of his more general efforts to adapt and grow.

Given the extremes of his behavior, the unpredictability of the shifts, and the diversity of his demands, it is reasonable to expect that his wife will experience a wide range of emotional reactions.

The wife of a forty-seven-year-old owner of a restaurant and cocktail lounge reacted to the change in pattern of their sexual relationship.

I'm no prude. I never kidded myself. I enjoy sex as much as he does. If I didn't, I never would have married him in the first place. I didn't go out with him for six months before we were married believing he was the kind of guy that wanted to hold hands in a library. That wasn't my style anyhow. I'm no intellectual. We've had a good sex life, but lately he's at me worse than when we were first married. The other day I was just coming home from shopping, and I see his car in the driveway. I ran into the house. Anything wrong? No, he's there grinning. Tells me he got an urge and came home. For God's sakes. Not now. I was supposed to go to the beauty shop. "Which is more important?" he asks me. I tried to tell him it's hard getting an appointment with the man who does my hair. In the middle of the day —two in the afternoon—he was ready to jump into bed. He blew up at me and left the house. Now he's going to show me. He told me I can just wait it out until he's ready. Here he tried to have a little fun with his own wife and she put him off. But that's how it's been going. I thought men his age slowed down. My husband is an exception. Feast or famine. I'm either worn out or edgy. I simply can't continue like this.

Faced with this kind of behavior, a wife may feel anger, disgust, dismay, frustration, astonishment—and occasionally, satisfaction, excitement, joy, and pleasure. When her husband is withdrawn and sexually seemingly dead, her efforts to arouse him often serve merely to increase his anxiety. Sometimes, despite the best of conscious intentions, her expressions of sympathetic concern reenforce his own worries about himself. When he becomes sexually hyperactive, and his wife doesn't share his enthusiasm for experimentation, he may feel rejected, and interpret her behavior as another threat to his virility. He may accuse her of getting old, being frigid, narrow-minded—and, of course, not understanding him.

Fathering

"They won't even ride a bicycle unless it has ten gears."

Up to this point in family life, the middle-forties male has probably been a normally attentive parent. Because of the demands of his work, he might not have been as closely and directly involved in the activities of his children as he would have wished, but he has probably been interested in their development, worried about their problems, delighted with their accomplishments. At this stage, however, the major focus of his concern turns inward, and he no longer has the psychic energy necessary for maintaining the same degree of interest in his children's day-to-day lives. It is not that he is uninterested in his children or loves them any the less, but he has his own psychological problems, and he is much less likely to become honestly involved in the issues facing his children at this time.

An electrical engineer in his middle forties reported his irritation with his wife's overinvolvement in their children.

When I was a kid you wouldn't catch my parents sitting at school plays, parents' meetings. Something's wrong nowadays. We've gone overboard on a kid-oriented culture. Kids can get through school, life, without parents breathing down their necks. I certainly did, and my parents had their own lives. They were damn good parents. None of us kids turned out badly.

But no—my wife insists we show up for every damn school function. One more production of *Our Town* by a high school amateur group and I'll stand up in the audience and tell them all to drop dead at the final burying scene. Enough is enough. How many times can I listen to jingle bells at Christmas time? I've been a kid. Why do I have to go through repeat performances? Look, I like the kids; they're good kids. Let them have their lives—me, I'm bored. I don't have to be in on everything. I don't want to hear about it and I don't see why I should have to relive it all.

His children's problems seem trivial in comparison to his own. They have almost their entire lifetime ahead of them, while he has probably lived well over half his life span. Their concerns seem so minor, so inconsequential, when he feels that his career is at stake, his marriage, his sense of himself as a man.

Sometimes he begins to suspect that his children create petty problems just to annoy him. He often feels that despite his best intentions as a father, his children simply don't have the strength of character that he himself had at their age; they've had it too easy, too soft, without the demands and frustrations he faced as a child. As a consequence, they are spoiled. The principal "spoiler," of course, has been his wife. If she had been firmer, a better disciplinarian, he wouldn't have to be burdened at his age with children who aren't strong enough to stand on their own two feet—and leave him alone to deal with his own problems. Thus, he reacts to the everyday problems of his children with boredom, growing irritation, and occasional outbursts of intense anger.

A forty-five-year-old service manager of an electrical appliance repair department talked about his children's demands.

I sit sometimes in the evening and wonder—what appreciation do my kids show me? Look at our style of living. A house, summer place, two cars, three TV's, an extension phone in every room. I ask myself, Do we need all this? I put in twenty hours some days; cut short vacations, and it adds up to more purchases—more to buy, more wants.

I'm no exception. There must be millions like our family. You know, in spite of all we have I can't see our lives as that much happier than when I was a kid. My family had nothing—believe me we had nothing. It was a big treat for me to get a dime to go with my kid brother to the movies. The manager charged a dime each if two sat in a seat. It cost fifteen cents to sit alone. I went through a childhood of Saturday movies on half a seat. Who had a bicycle? Now my kids need cars. They won't even ride a bicycle unless it has ten gears. After all, how can you go up hills? What hills? This isn't the Alps. Where we live the streets are flatter than pancakes. What do they need ten gears for? I resent the fact that I let myself be caught, dragged into a net of more and more. I'd give a lot to be sitting on half a seat for a four-hour double feature on Saturday afternoon.

If the children are adolescents at this time, his relationships with them are even further complicated by the fact that they are living through their own crisis of identity. They too are concerned with the question "Who Am I?" and they too are engaged in a period of experimentation, trial and error. As part of their own process of psychological development, they are questioning the values and behaviors of their childhood, trying out new roles, new points of view. They too are unsure of themselves, and as a consequence, likely to be dogmatic, hypercritical of adults, and aggressively assertive. Interactions between father and adolescent, then, become a tinderbox. Neither is likely to be very sensitive to or sympathetic with the problems experienced by the other; both are egocentrically involved in their own developmental crises.

The relationship with a late-adolescent son frequently has an especially intense emotional tone. In almost all instances, the basis for this emotional intensity is largely unconscious, with neither father nor son aware of why their relationship has become so explosive. The problem has its roots in a conflict that, in some respects, is the mirror image of the Oedipal relationship they had lived through so many years before. When the son was young, he was obviously and unequivocally the weaker male. Therefore, in any rivalry with his father, for his mother's attention or anything else, it was primarily the son who felt threatened and who inhibited or repressed any impulse to compete openly and aggressively. At this stage, the situation has changed, and to some extent the roles are reversed. The father in his middle forties is particularly concerned about his own apparently waning virility. He may feel flabby, tired, worried about his health, and anxious about his sexual drive, desirability, and performance. At the same time, his adolescent son's virility is becoming increasingly obvious—even blatant. It is now the father who feels the pangs of jealousy, the threat of imagined or potential competition. In this limited sense, it is the Oedipus complex in reverse, with a youthful, vigorous son, and a father who sees himself becoming weaker and less potent.

The wife of a forty-six-year-old architect described the dilemma she faced acting as a mediator between her son and her husband.

I don't remember how it started. All I know is the kids were out in the backyard with my husband. They seemed to be playing some game, and then the wrestling started. My husband and our oldest son, who is fifteen, were fooling around. Our son is very strong now and almost as big as his father. I think he must have said something about how he could pin my husband to the ground. I'm not sure. All I know is the two of them went at each other. It started out as fun. Then it seemed to be serious. I tried to stop them. My husband became furious, screamed at me—told me to get the hell back in the house. Then he said to my son, "You think you're stronger?" Or something like that.

The boy wanted to quit. I could tell that from his face. But my husband kept at him, calling him scared. He dared the boy to beat him. They went at each other. The younger ones came into the house crying. Even they knew something was wrong. I went out again to stop them. There wasn't anything I could do. He had the boy on the ground with his arms twisted.

"So you're stronger?" He kept repeating the words. It didn't even sound like my husband's voice. The boy cried, and that did it. He was allowed to get up. He went into his room and stayed there—wouldn't come out to dinner—wouldn't let me in. I kept begging him to let me in, and I would talk to him. He said he didn't want to talk to me or to his father ever again.

I asked my husband, "Why?" He said the boy had been at him he was stronger. Well, it was about time he learned who was stronger. He was tired of the kid pulling this threat. It was a lesson. I wasn't to go up to the boy's room again. I was to stay out of it.

I was in the middle—a son or a husband. I went up anyway and talked. I have never seen the boy's face that bruised, and he had marks on his arms. He told me he had been only kidding, and Dad had taken him seriously. My husband said the boy had to be taught a lesson; that he was becoming impossible, and as long as the boy lived in the house he had to know who was the father and who was the son. I asked if the only way he could teach him respect was with his fists. I said there had to be another way. My husband said no. The boy wouldn't understand—they had to have it out. It was weeks before they faced each other without glaring.

The intrapsychic pressures felt by the middle-forties husband and father are enormous. He is unsure of who he is, where he is going. He needs an opportunity to try himself out; he needs freedom from external demands. As we have mentioned, during adolescence, a stage of development in which the individual has similar needs, there is often a period of moratorium—a withdrawal from external demands and outside pressures, a turning inward in search of self. If he is still in school, the adolescent for a time may seem to "float," apparently unconcerned with the day-to-day routines of study. If he is out of school, he may travel with no explicit aim or purpose, just wandering from place to place without seeming to care much about where he is. Or he may take a job that is totally incongruent with his previous interests, training, or talents—a job whose main attraction is that it permits him to work without at all involving himself. For a time he can live in a different world, untouched by the normal demands of his society.

The man caught in the middle-forties crisis may yearn for the same kind of cocoon-like withdrawal, but for him, the demands of reality are likely to be much too compelling. There are bills to be paid, donations to give, duties that must be fulfilled. He cannot comfortably withdraw from the responsibilities he has acquired over the past twenty years. He cannot take off to bum around Europe; he can't float through his daily work.

As a result, he naturally experiences an even greater sense of frustration. Suffering the pangs of inner conflict and the stresses of external threat, he feels blocked in his efforts to escape. He is frustrated by the demands of everyday living, and the frustration inevitably evokes aggression. True enough, at one time he willingly, even eagerly, took on the responsibilities of children, a family, a career. But now these responsibilities are barriers to freedom, the freedom he needs to adapt and grow. Thus, he is frustrated and angry, sometimes at himself, but more often at the person closest to him, his wife, who comes to represent all of the chains —economic, moral, social—that bind him to the routines of his daily life.

A forty-six-year-old chemist for a drug firm reacted to a multitude of home problems which continually confronted him.

There's a real difference between people in the outside world and my family. I go home to my wife, and the first thing she greets me with is some problem. There are squirrels in the roof. We have to call an exterminator—thirty-five bucks for every pair of squirrels he catches. One night it's squirrels; the next night the water heater is broken; a toilet needs fixing. I told her, "If you want a repairman for a husband,

why the hell didn't you marry one?" I work hard.
I see the difference at the office. Last week a few of
us went out for a drink. We sat around the table, four
of us—Ginny, my secretary, another guy and his secretary. We felt alive. We talked about art, the theater.
I laughed. It's been a long time since I felt like laughing. There was nothing that went on—believe me—
but that night I got home late, and I open the door and
it was like a cold-water bath. My wife tells me two
thousand bucks for the orthodontist—she just got the
report that day—and a garage window was broken. The
kids were playing ball in the driveway. You know, I had
just come back from something very different. I stood
there looking at her, and I felt I never wanted to see
her or the kids again.

Playing Around

"It's not sex only—we talk."

Given the strains and stresses of his family life, it is not at
all surprising that the middle-forties husband begins to
search more frequently for companionship and satisfaction
outside the home. Indeed, there is often a sharp increase in
extramarital experiences, which include nonsexual as well as
sexual relationships. This phenomenon is commonly recognized in the folklore of our society, and is a ready source of
popular humor. However, the man going through this phase
doesn't find these jokes very funny. As a matter of fact, these

relationships are most often characterized by an earnest, almost solemn emotional tone that clearly contradicts the popular view of the philanderer joyfully jumping in and out of beds.

A pathologist, forty-five years of age, portrayed his entire married life as a twenty-year period of hell. Recently, he has started living with a co-worker, someone who he believes can share his life after the divorce is final.

Twenty years ago when I married my wife I knew she was different from me—different interests. I kidded myself that it wouldn't matter. It took me about a week to realize my mistake. Twenty years of hell and boredom. I compromised myself—ended up with two lives. One at work, the other a fake. It didn't do any good to try and talk about what I did with my wife. She doesn't understand and couldn't understand if she tried.

I've reached an age where I've had enough of marking time. I want more than a bed partner when I leave the lab. I want intellectual companionship—someone who understands my work. Elizabeth is my lab assistant. A relationship developed—believe me, it wasn't Elizabeth. She resisted—told me she wasn't going to get involved with a married man with kids. It was me after her. We've been going out to dinner. I didn't only want to go to bed. We just talked. I finally persuaded her last month that I was serious. I told Elizabeth she isn't breaking up anything—there's nothing to break up. My marriage is over and done with.

I've taken an apartment in the city. I stay there during the week and try to get home to see the kids on Saturday and Sunday. When the divorce is final, Elizabeth and I'll get married. Twenty years in a big lie. I'm getting out, and I've never felt so good about anything.

As one might expect, the behavior and needs of the middle-forties man are especially incongruent and seemingly contradictory. On the one hand, he may accuse his wife of being old-fashioned, a bore, and insensitive. On the other hand, he needs her reassurance, her flattery, her total acceptance and encouragement. He wants her to recognize and take seriously his feelings of weakness, doubt, insecurity; at the same time he wants her to treat him as a strong, sensitive, and powerful man.

Needless to say, it is virtually impossible for any woman to fulfill this role while at the same time serving as the principal target of her husband's resentment, sarcasm, and anger. It is unreasonable to expect a wife to respond to hostility with sweet, loving kindness. Thus the husband's aggression leads to his wife's counter-aggression. They bicker, complain, nag; they hurt each other as only those who have loved and lived together for a long time can. They know each other's particular weaknesses and hidden fears, and these become the targets of attack in battles that sometimes reach extraordinary heights of viciousness. As a result, the marital relationship is severely strained. Under these conditions, it becomes increasingly likely that the middle-forties husband will venture outside of marriage to satisfy his needs for psychological support. Add to this the attraction of novelty, plus the potential thrill of adventure, and it is not difficult to understand the increased frequency of extramarital affairs at this stage.

A forty-six-year-old editor of a trade magazine expressed irritation with his wife's failure to be responsive. He contrasted her lack of interest with reactions he elicited in the outside world.

> You know, I feel like a doormat in my own house. And you know what happens eventually to doormats—they wear out. This doormat is wearing thin. My wife sees me as someone who brings home money—period. Sure,

I come in and she says, "How was your day?" I said to
her last night, "You ask me how was my day. Why in
the hell don't you shut up and let me answer?" She sees
me as a fixture in the house. Someday I'm going to tell
her—outside in the world people notice me.

Let me give you an example. I bought a jacket—
O.K., it wasn't the greatest jacket in the world; the
fabric was so-so, but it was a damn nice-looking jacket.
You think anyone in my house noticed the jacket? No
—but at the office it took one of the typists from the
typing pool to say something. She wasn't out to flatter
me. I don't pay her salary. I didn't hire her. She doesn't
owe me anything. I happened to see her in the afternoon and she said to me, "Mr. Eherns, I think your
jacket is gorgeous." Now, I ask, if *she* can take the time
and trouble for no ulterior motive to stop and notice
my jacket, then why can't my own wife who I've been
married to for twenty-three years do the same?

To a large extent, the middle-aged husband's choice
for the role of "other woman" depends upon who is
available in his daily life. He is often busy, tired, ob-
sessed with his own problems, and he usually doesn't
have the time or energy to search very far afield. The
women he encounters at work most likely see him as
strong, capable, and mature. They sincerely appreciate
him, respect him, maybe even fear him a bit, which certainly doesn't hurt his ego. They know how hard he
works, know the everyday problems he must face, and
most important, they are *there*, close by, available. Moreover, they never mention the orthodontist bills, the leak-
ing faucets, the thousand petty details of daily family
life. They are appreciative, admiring, accepting, flattering, undemanding—a ready source of ego balm. Little
wonder, then, that the relationship between the middle-
forties husband and the women he works with sometimes

goes beyond what is called for under normal working conditions.

A thirty-four-year-old private secretary to a financial executive in his mid-forties talked about their relationship.

I really tried to discourage him. He asked me out a month after I started to work for him. I wasn't all fired up about getting involved. I knew he was married, had kids. I hardly saw myself as a marriage breaker. But is it my fault his wife and he aren't getting along? I certainly didn't start the trouble. I'm only in on the tail end. I told him, "You're married—I don't want to play around." He told me it's only playing around if he was married in the "real sense." He doesn't have a married life. He made a mistake. He was forced to marry her. She used a baby as an excuse. That was before abortion was easy, but she probably wouldn't have had one anyhow, she was so bent on catching him. He said he didn't even know her well—was just caught. He had just come back from the army—that was 1950.

He's a darling boss—a dear. I mean, when you get tired and you're all dragged out he just says, "Take the day off." I wouldn't dream of taking advantage of him. He's just so intelligent and knows so much. I can't imagine ever keeping up with him. He's very sensitive. That's why it's so awful thinking that this poor bewildered kid just out of the army let himself get caught by some woman. You'd think she would have realized how terrible it was—if he didn't love her. How could she go ahead and marry him? Marriage is two ways.

When I get serious about someone I don't want it to be one-sided. I've told him how I feel. I said I'm not the kind of woman who's just a good-time gal. Any guy I get tied up with at my age has to meet me halfway. He understands. Right now it's sort of hanging. We go out steadily. I feel sorry for the kids, but they're not babies. I could never do this if he had little kids. I finally told him, "Look, I can't go on like this—one foot in the door—either we go the whole way and get married or forget it." I'm just not going to be any married guy's mistress even if he's super—like my boss.

This is not the only direction the husband's wanderings can take. Sometimes he looks around closer to home, noticing a neighbor's or friend's wife. She may be someone he has known for years, and except for an occasional fantasy, a person with whom he has had only the most proper social relations. Suddenly, she seems more attractive and attracting, somehow sexier and intriguing. Perhaps she has been suffering with a mid-forties male in her house and is eager for a relationship that doesn't involve the bickering and hostility she has recently encountered in her own marriage. Instead of a man who accuses her of being ignorant, nagging, and sexually boring, she finds someone who feels she is exciting, interesting, and fun to be with. She in turn can be warm, accepting, reassuring, coquettish, lively, humorous —all those things she once was with her own husband before he became a touchy, explosive, demanding bull in their once-quiet bedroom.

A forty-five-year-old owner of a dental laboratory voiced resentment against his wife, whom he saw as aging. In contrast, he was experiencing a surge of new interests and youthful vitality.

My wife is ready for a rocking chair—a front-porch swing. I'm not. The fact is, I haven't aged physically. She has. She feels old—I don't. I'm not ready to throw in the sponge and sit on some hotel verandah nursing aches and pains. I feel good—alive. I've got time and money to take up some things I never had the opportunity for when I was younger.

I can't get her to go along. I bought this boat. I like

to sail on weekends. Out there on the water, on a good day—there's nothing like it. I dive off the side, take a swim—my whole body feels good. My wife won't put one foot on the boat. She says it's tiring. She'd rather do other things. "Like what," I ask, "sitting on a front-porch rocker?" I like to do these things with people. She's given me no choice. I just went ahead and invited a few friends last Saturday. We had a great time. One of the women who's come along this past month really made me think about my wife. Her husband is the same. Hates boats. This gal loved the boat. Wants to come out again. She caught on, right off, to everything I showed her. It hit me that it's not just women in general who complain. It's my wife.

Or perhaps his stumbling leads him across the path of a much younger woman, someone who has always felt more comfortable with "mature men." Maybe she is bored by the sexual, psychological, vocational floundering of her male peers, and is attracted by men of a certain fatherly age and stature. Thus, the mid-forties professor meets the young female student who is enthralled by his discovery of fossils from the early paleolithic age; the doctor encounters the recent nursing-school graduate who "really understands the stress of holding life in the palm of my hand." And stock-brokers, bankers, lawyers, businessmen, and teachers discover the sensitivity and warmth of young women who once seemed so young, but suddenly seem so mature and understanding.

Twenty-three years of age, an emergency-room nurse talked about her relationship with one of the doctors. She was resentful that his wife refused to agree to a divorce.

I saw his wife with him one day. Honestly, I wonder what he ever saw in her in the first place. She was wearing a tweed coat she must have bought in some thrift shop. Her hair was straggly—the ends all frizzled. She didn't have on any make-up. She could have been his mother. That's how old she looked. I can understand now a lot of things he's been telling me. He said he hasn't been to bed with her in three years. She knows he's seeing someone else. What does she think he does staying away three nights a week? But every time he brings up a divorce she says she won't give him one. I don't know why she wants to hang on like that. He told me he doesn't want to go ahead without her consent because of the children. But he doesn't owe her anything. You'd think she'd know he doesn't care for her any more. It's an empty relationship. He goes there Wednesdays and Saturdays for dinner and comes right back to my place. He's just drained. He says she told him she will fight giving him up. We can't live on my salary, and the way she talks she's going to wring every cent he's got. I don't understand a woman like that. If it were me, I would say O.K., get out. They're shells to each other. He told me he doesn't even know why he married her in the first place—just fell into it. It's not that they've been having this marvelous marriage and suddenly it's all over. We're very much in love, and I'm not going to give him up. He won't leave me. I know that for sure.

It is all too easy to make jokes about these extramarital affairs—about bosses and their secretaries, about the middle-aged man with the girl fresh out of adolescence. "My wife doesn't understand me," for example, has become a litany from which have flowed countless cartoons and cracks about the extramarital activities of the middle-forties man. But for those involved, it is no joking matter. As we have indicated earlier, these affairs are often pursued with a profound intensity and seriousness. It is rarely a matter of two people simply out to enjoy some sexual fun and games. We do not mean to minimize the sexual aspect, but it is important to understand that these extramarital affairs are not *primarily* a matter of sexual play. More often, they are characterized by a striving for a sense of authenticity and in-depth understanding. The sex is generally not pursued with a happy-go-lucky, devil-may-care attitude. Rather, it is integral to a process of mutual exploration that is psychological as well as physical. For the man in his middle forties, it is part of an almost desperate search for himself reflected in another person.

An airline pilot told about separating from his wife of twenty-four years. Approaching a forty-seventh birthday, he felt young and elated.

Breaking loose from my wife was the smartest move I've made. I didn't think I could do it. Not because I didn't want to, but she threatened and held on. I thought she had me there for a while—caught by every gimmick you can imagine. It took a while for her to see I meant business. We were through. I moved downstairs this past year. That made her mad. Nothing she could do. She tried and I laughed her off. It was over between us. She had enough and we went through the divorce. I haven't felt so alive in years.

The kids are grown. They don't need me. They never saw me as much else other than a checkbook anyhow. There's nothing like freedom. No one to answer to. I don't have to report in and out. I'm my own boss. It's the first time I've been independent since I was in the service. I'm discovering I'm not the dog my wife saw.

Women take an interest in me. They aren't like my wife. I'm surprised sometimes. I realize I had been shut off for so many years. You would have thought the old ones would be out after your skin as a last chance. That's not the case. Young women today are different

—more mature. This stewardess and I have been seeing a little of each other. Nothing serious yet, but I can talk to her. She has respect for my opinions. She's not just a sponge sitting there—reacts. Her interest in me as a person made me stop and think. It's not sex only—we talk. She has real know-how, a sense of what's what. I come away after an evening satisfied—no strain, no acting. She's a very straight person. Sure she's young, but that doesn't matter. She told me she always got along better with older men. Young guys wouldn't appreciate her. I can see that. She's a very unusual person.

Thus, far from a joking matter, the extramarital experiences of the middle-forties man are a product of the intrapsychic stresses he encounters in the normal course of his development and the interpersonal conditions these stresses engender. They stem from his own fears and self-doubts, and the marital difficulties arising from this internal confusion. They are certainly not a return to adolescence. No adolescent could very long bear the deadly serious sense of purpose with which the man in his middle forties is likely to engage in his love affairs. Although there is something of the same egocentric quality about the ventures of the adolescent and the older man, the man in his middle forties has probably acquired some interpersonal skills that at least mask the more blatantly egocentric concerns. In comparison to the adolescent, he is both more sophisticated and more frightened, more sensitive and more selfish, more controlled and more guilt-ridden, more powerful and more anxious about his power. He is not out for a moment's titillation; he is in search of himself, a self he feels he has somehow lost in the course of life.

The Game of Work

*"I hear colleagues of mine talking about medical
practice as if it were the automobile business."*

The initial reaction of the man in his early forties to threat
and disappointment in his work is to work even harder,
spend longer hours and more energy in his effort to achieve
the long-term goals of his career. After a while, however,
when his efforts do not lead to any apparent change, he
begins to feel that the additional expenditure of time and
energy is simply digging a deeper rut from which he will
never be able to escape. The goals he once thought were so
close at hand become increasingly distant, and he becomes
disenchanted.

He reacts to this disenchantment in a variety of ways, the
most common of which are aggression and avoidance. His
aggression is manifested by an increasingly cynical view of
both his work and those engaged in it. For example, in
discussing his work, he may more frequently use words like
"game" or "racket," implying that it is something less than
the serious pursuit that others consider it to be. In talking
about success in the "game," he may emphasize the importance of luck, contacts, willingness to break a few rules now
and then. And when he refers to those who are engaged in
the "racket," he is more apt to use words like "operators"
or "con-men," and sometimes even "fakers" or "crooks."

In making these comments, he is usually not overtly hostile. At this point he is probably not even aware of his own
hostility. He is likely to believe that he is merely being open
and honest about something he knows, dropping his professional mask, "telling it like it is."

A forty-seven-year-old physician reflected cynicism about
some members of his profession.

I'm not arguing for practice without fees. Of course, I expect to be paid for services. But it's gotten out of hand. I hear colleagues of mine, some of the same people I went to school with, talking about practice as if it were the automobile business. The fact is it isn't. I didn't go into medicine for a "fast dollar." Too many years without earning a dime. If money were the only goal there must be quicker and faster ways. Somewhere along the line some of my classmates lost their ideals. I don't think I am as guilty. I really don't. I haven't got a yacht, an expensive car. I do well. I can't deny that, but I haven't compromised every principle I started out with. Others have. They talk about operations in terms of cash register receipts—not what they are treating, but how much they are charging. When you start tying in an operation directly to the dollar, there are problems. I know some men who deliberately push for big money operations. These kind of people have put medicine into the position of any "shakedown racket." These kind of people go a long way towards hurting a lot of us who still care.

In the real world of work, of course, there is no job, no profession that doesn't have its seamier, less attractive side. Therefore, such a man is not being consciously dishonest or deceptive. He is probably being partially accurate about something he knows very well, and he may even feel a kind of masochistic satisfaction in his cynical truth-telling. Undoubtedly, luck does play a part in professional success; personal contacts certainly don't hurt; and on some occasions, willingness to break some rules might be an asset.

But in his growing dissatisfaction and disenchantment, he sometimes fails to recognize that the more unsavory side of work reflects only one dimension of reality. In any event, the ethics of the world of work is not at all our concern here. More important for our purposes is understanding the behavior of the mid-forties man in terms of the crisis through which he is living. From this point of view, his critical comments, his more or less overt hostility make perfectly good psychological sense. In part, the behaviors are the aggressive consequences of his frustration. He has invested a great deal of himself, his talents, time, and energy in the career he has pursued for many years. A central part of his adult identity has been defined by the nature of that work. By this time in his life, he may well have gained a good deal of reward from this investment—money, status, power, a sense of competence. But he may also feel that the ultimate goals toward which he has been working, the really important peaks of success, have eluded him. Now, as the upward momentum of his career has slowed, perhaps even stopped, he feels frustrated and angry, and the anger is expressed in the cynical terms with which he talks about his work.

This cynicism is also a preamble to withdrawal and avoidance. One of the major problems faced by many men during their thirties and early forties is overinvolvement in their work. Many of them do not experience it as *over*involvement; perhaps that term more aptly describes their families' opinions or views. At any rate, however it is labeled, the typical thirty-five-year-old man is often so taken up with the demands of work that he hardly has time or energy available for other aspects of his life. This pattern continues into the early forties, sometimes to an even greater degree than before, with more and more time and energy focused on his career. But then, as his frustration increases, he begins to withdraw from a position of total investment of himself.

This withdrawal may take many forms. For example, in the past, whatever he did, wherever he was, thoughts about his work seemed to occupy him continuously—not only on the job, but at home, on vacation, on the golf course, at parties, even in bed. But now, the reverse may be his problem. While he is at work, he may find it difficult to keep his mind focused on the job he is supposed to be doing. He daydreams about a trip he has thought of taking. In the middle of the working day his mind drifts from one subject to another—fantasies of the past, the future—wandering aimlessly from topic to topic, with no common theme except that most of what he tends to think about is unrelated to his day-to-day work.

A forty-six-year-old chief auditor for an insurance company talked about recent experiences with lapses in concentration.

It bothers me lately when I drift off. I'm the kind of person who was always seen as having a "one-track mind." If I was working on a job, the building could cave in on top of me for all I cared. Now sometimes I get an idea in my head—nothing to do with work— and it sticks. I was at a meeting the other day—an investment report meeting, and I'm sitting there looking like I'm listening. All the while in my head I see myself at this resort. Went there last winter. Some island deal. Tremendous food. You name it—they had it. I got hooked on sailing those Sunfishes. I've been thinking about getting one. They don't cost too much, and you can haul them around on a trailer.

The meeting—well maybe the guys wondered because I didn't have much to say. They're carrying on about investment plans, and I'm sitting in the sun with this Sunfish. I'd like to go back around there soon. I've been spending a lot of time thinking about it. It's a great place, and I better make reservations.

His avoidance maneuvers may not be limited to the realm of fantasy. At one time it may have been difficult to get him talking very long about anything unrelated to his work. Art, music, community affairs—they were important, of course, and he would probably listen politely for a while. But sooner or later his conversation would return to the immediate concerns in his career. If he was practicing law, he felt most at home talking with other lawyers; if he sold insurance, his conversations in one way or another led to policies, rates, and dividends.

But now he may find himself talking less and less about anything related to his work. Yes, he does sell stocks or manufacture dresses or design bathrooms or publish books —but he would much rather talk about his golf game, a new fiber-glass tennis racket, a trip to Central America, his garden.

The avoidance techniques often go beyond fantasy and conversation. The mid-forties man may in fact actually begin to spend less time on his regular job, and become more involved in other activities. He is likely to come up with various schemes to make money in ways that are totally divorced from his career, and sometimes he may pursue these schemes with considerable enthusiasm.

The manager of a coffeehouse talked about his three bosses, all of whom were actively involved in the business.

I must have been nuts to take this job. But I've been in the restaurant business for twenty years. I can't afford to own my own place. So I go to work for these three psychos [psychiatrists]. They got big offices. Their patients come here all the time. I could tell you some real stories about the people we get sitting in here, but that's something else.

Three of them put up the money. I get a good salary, believe me, no complaints. But you can't run a coffeehouse with three bosses whose experience in the business has been they like to drink coffee. I mean, who needs that? One tells me over the phone, did I clean out the urns? The other tells me to check some catalogue because he knows about a new espresso machine that makes better espresso than the one we got with less coffee. He saw it in Italy. He goes to Italy and gets the idea we need a new machine.

I got one here in the morning, one at noon, and one in the evening. They go in the kitchen and they start getting in the way. I can't tell them not to. It's their place. But Jesus, they got big practices. I bet my rock bottom dollar they aren't listening to their patients. They sit there thinking of espresso machines and coffee beans. One's going nuts with some kind of pastry—he wants the cook to learn how to make it. Money or not, I don't know if I can last with the three of them in here every day, and when they're not in they're on the telephone.

Within the framework of his own career, the middle-forties professional may also exhibit a good deal of restless experimentation. For example, a doctor who has been in general practice may begin thinking about specializing in one field or another; the professor may begin to think about the attractions of being a dean; a lawyer begins thinking of becoming a judge. In each case, there is a shaking loose from habitual patterns of behavior, a search for new ways of working and living. It is a time of active exploration, of trials and errors—occasionally compounded by further errors. It is also a time of excitement, promise, novelty. Within the stirrings of discontent are the seeds of change and growth.

The Seriousness of Games

"He's gone bananas with this tennis."

As a younger man, he didn't have much time to play. He was busy building his career, and after all, "play is for kids." However, in the middle-forties, the picture changes considerably. He begins to play with great enthusiasm and energy. He may become a part-time painter, potter, or musician; he may become an avid camper, golfer, sailor, or mountain hiker. Whatever he does, he is likely to do it with remarkable intensity and devotion.

The mid-forties man's play is motivated by a number of complex, interrelated factors. At the most obvious level, play is fun. If he is engaged in some form of athletics, he may enjoy a sense of skill in the activity and the thrill of competition. If he turns to sculpting, he may experience great pleasure in the tactile sensations of working with clay or stone. Thus, regardless of what other motives might be operating, enjoyment of the activity itself is a primary component of his motivation to play.

Closely related to the hedonistic motivation is his sense of rewarding himself. He has worked hard for years, often going for long stretches of time with little or no vacation. At this stage, he begins to feel that most of the tangible rewards for his work have gone to support the play of others, usually his children, and now he feels it is his turn. Instead of worrying about saving enough money to send the kids to summer camp, he becomes more concerned with getting together the money to take a Caribbean cruise—without the children. After all, he has sacrificed, scrounged, and saved; it is time for some self-reward before it is too late to enjoy it.

At another level, the involvement in play may represent

part of his private argument with aging. This is particularly true for those whose middle-aged play is principally athletic —the tennis players, golfers, skiers, and others who display a marked resurgence in a variety of athletic activities. The logic of this internal argument includes a number of related facets. For example, he may be reaffirming an implicit belief that, given enough regular exercise, he can regain and retain the physical vigor of earlier days. His ability to run around a tennis court for two hours or play twenty-seven holes of golf can serve as proof that he is still a healthy male. It would be naïve to assume that he is trying to recapture his youth. This is a common oversimplification that hardly does justice to the complexity of his motivation. He is well aware that he is no longer eighteen years old, and in any event, it is unlikely that he would choose to live through that difficult age again. His aim is not to regress to his youth, but rather to demonstrate to himself and others that middle forties is an age of masculine strength.

The wife of a forty-six-year-old marketing analyst spoke candidly about her husband's surge of physical activity, which she feels is potentially dangerous for a man his age.

I can't say he's not in good shape. He has the body of a much younger man. All the women at the club are surprised when I tell them my husband is in his middle forties. But he's gone bananas with this tennis. He keeps going for four hours. His back kills him but he won't admit it. He goes and sits in the club steam room and then falls out of the door exhausted. When he comes home he goes to sleep. I tell him one hour like a sane person is enough. But no—not him. He makes out like he was twenty. Now they're having a club tournament, and he goes out to practice at dawn on Sundays. It's madness. His body can't take it. So he'll win the geriatrics olympics—he should be so lucky. I'll put the trophy over his grave. Seriously, you should see him with ace bandages on his knees, more bandages on his wrists, and now he tells me he has a tennis elbow, so he's started cortisone shots. My friend's husband who plays with Al says she knows someday she'll get a telephone call from the club pro to come pick up her husband. She's sure he'll have a heart attack on the court. She says there's no reasoning with him to cut down—no way.

There is another, less obvious, dimension of motivation more central to his psychological crisis. During this period, the middle-forties male is breaking out of the ruts of his past life, experimenting with new behaviors. And it is on the fields of play—the tennis court, the golf course—that he can rehearse new aspects of a changing identity. Most important, he can try himself out in settings and situations that are divorced from the practical demands of his life. In comparison to home or office, play provides a setting that is relatively safe for psychological trial and error. Thus, if he has been a cautious, careful person up to now, on the tennis courts he can try out a bolder, more radical identity. He can shake loose from earlier inhibitions at the painting easel, experiment with aloneness and test the limits of his endurance on a mountain trail, try a more dashing personal style as captain of his sailboat. In a sense, play serves as the setting for a middle-forties moratorium, a setting in which he can withdraw for a time from the demands of the everyday world, and search for himself.

Given this complex pattern of interrelated motives, one can readily appreciate the intensity with which the mid-forties male pursues his play. Just as he once pursued goals of work with sincere devotion, so too may he now pursue the goals of play with earnest dedication. While it may be true that mere playful play is really just for kids, play in the middle forties is a serious and important business.

The interest in the new sport is rarely limited to the actual field of play. For example, he is likely to be a most active buyer of equipment. The tennis-playing middle-forties male probably has a wooden racket or two, another one made of metal, and he has been looking at a fiber-glass model that has just come on the market. If he's a sailor, his opportunities for buying equipment are nearly limitless—a machine to determine the depth of water, another to locate fish, still another to navigate by radio signals; charts, pennants, ropes, polishes, hooks, anchors—the list is splendidly endless.

He not only enjoys the sport of buying equipment, he also loves to talk about his particular play activity. He is likely to have learned a great deal about it and probably has formed some strong opinions. Sharing this knowledge becomes an important part of his overall play activity, sometimes even more satisfying than the sport itself.

The wife of a lawyer, nearing his forty-seventh birthday, reported her reactions to her husband's involvement with scuba-diving equipment.

Last winter we were in the Caribbean for a vacation. My husband took scuba-diving lessons. The first one was free on the package deal we had, the rest he paid for. When we came home he wanted to get his own equipment. Said it was cheaper to buy all he needed instead of renting it. I asked him how often he was going to go scuba diving. He said that wasn't the point. He'd have the gear when we went. That started it. I think we have every catalogue in the world that sells equipment. One week he orders a mask; the next, fins, a tank. Then he decided the tank he got was too small. He could only go down one thousand feet—don't ask me—but whatever, he decided he needs a bigger tank. Go down to our basement. We have equipment enough to dive around the whole Atlantic ocean. He won't tell me the costs so far. I think he's embarrassed. Now, the worst is that I don't think we can go back to the Caribbean this year. Besides, he's got some high blood pressure—nothing serious—but I told him I'm not going to be a widow simply because he wants to dress up in a black wet suit with a helmet on his head. The closest he's going to get to water this year is the bathtub.

An Attack of Vanity

"They want style . . . vents, plaids, gold buttons, hot pink shirts."

One of the major forces initiating the crisis of the early forties was a growing awareness of personal mortality and accompanying signs of physical aging. The man in his early forties reacted to this threat with anxiety, but by the middle forties he has recovered from the initial shock and responds actively and energetically.

This response does not represent a denial of his mortality. In general, by the mid-forties, he tends to be realistic about these facts of life, and rejection of the undeniable is not one of his favored modes of defense. Day follows day and year follows year, no matter what he does to the calendar. Thus, rather than kid himself about the fact of his chronological age, he engages in a variety of activities designed to deal with the side effects of aging. He may, for example, decide that now is the time to lose the five, ten, or fifteen pounds he has acquired over the years. As a consequence, he is a prime candidate for any of the various diets that happen to be popular. Along the same line, he may for a time become a glutton for exercise—jogging, bicycling, hiking, or going through a routine of push-ups, knee bends, and sit-ups.

Accompanying his heightened interest in physical well-being is a growing concern with his appearance. While he may not become a man of fashion, in more or less subtle ways his style of dress does change.

A young clothing salesman in a men's wear store commented on the tastes of the middle-aged clientele.

I've seen it a thousand times. They start swinging when they're pushing up near fifty. Want style. They come in here wearing conservative cuts, dark gray and blue, and they walk out with vents, plaids, gold buttons, hot pink shirts. I had one guy in here this morning—looked like a VP; he was in a gray flannel suit, white shirt, cuff links. You'll never believe me when I tell you he walks out of here in a turtleneck, bell trousers, a jacket that I couldn't unload on a teenager at half the price. You should have seen the plaid. He asks me how does he look. You make a two-hundred buck sale; the guy is standing there, with a paunch, gray hair, bags under his eyes and what do you say? You tell me.

There is no style that belongs uniquely to the middle-forties male, but in general, his clothes become more colorful, more up-to-date. He may explore a variety of styles, in clothes as well as general appearance. For example, he may try a mustache or sideburns, a beard, longer hair, bow ties, ascots, leather jackets, turtleneck sweaters. The specific changes are hardly important; the process of change is crucial, for it mirrors externally his inner search.

Shifting Values

"My beliefs and values are on quicksand, and I'd give a lot for some firm ground."

When he was going through the identity crisis of his late teens and early twenties, the man who is now in his middle forties developed an ideology—a set of beliefs, attitudes, and values that guided his understanding of the world. The terms of his ideology may have been primarily political, scientific, or religious; the ideology may have been implicit in his behavior rather than explicitly stated. But regardless of the specific terms or the degree to which it was consciously formulated, this system of beliefs provided a framework within which he made sense of his life for the next quarter of a century. It was the philosophical bedrock of his day-to-day life. But then, as his sense of identity is shaken in the period of his early forties, so too is the ideological foundation of this identity disturbed and disrupted.

Threatened by self-doubt, the middle-forties man also begins to doubt the beliefs that once helped him make sense of the world he lives in. The dyed-in-the-wool socialist begins to resent government control of his life. The devout church member begins to question the wisdom of his religion. The dedicated scientist begins to wonder whether a scientific point of view can ever provide answers to questions about life that are becoming increasingly important to him.

An elementary school principal, forty-seven years of age, talked about a shift in values triggered off by an incident that occurred with his son.

People my age grew up in a time when you didn't question the world like the kids do now. I can think back on my own life. I went into service—right out of high school. You didn't talk back. You were conditioned to obey. I came back from the war, went to college, graduate school—and I conformed. My father drummed it into me. He used to say, "You'll never beat the system by talking back." My whole life has been this way. Take my job now—a principal in an elementary school in a conservative town. I wouldn't have kept this job one day if I were any different. That's a fact. I was nearly fired a few years ago. I went before town committees fighting for my position because my son wasn't like his father. He was a draft resister. He was *not* going to go to Vietnam. His picture was in every local paper. I got telephone calls at night. My wife was asked to quit the library committee. It didn't matter that I had a Purple Heart, believed in the system, had fought for the system. It was my son or my job. But more than that, my son kept talking to me. I stood behind him. Why didn't he have a right to his own views? The least I could do was back him, though at first I thought he was wrong; he should serve his turn. It was rough going for me, for him, and the rest of the family. Then all this political business has come out. And I'm not sure I have the answers. I was wrong with my son. The recent political scandals shook me up. I'm not certain any more about lots of things. Even religion. I told my wife we go to church every Sunday, and we have been following rules. Maybe those rules aren't for everyone. Maybe I don't feel like believing any more just because people have believed one way for thousands of years. It's one thing, then another—like a house with a cracking foundation. Only one way to go—the cracks get wider.

There is rarely an overnight revolution in the thinking of the middle-forties man. He does not abruptly reject the perspective, the beliefs, attitudes, and values he has lived with for so many years. Instead, there is a gradual process that develops over time, an accrual of doubt that often begins with trivial matters of everyday life. At first there is little understanding of the eventual magnitude of the ideological crisis that is beginning. But the trivial doubt remains unresolved, often below the level of awareness. Then, one moment of doubt leads to another—and another—eventually breaking into consciousness. It is at this point that the middle-forties man becomes a philosopher, for with doubt there is the beginning of reflective thought.

The key issue of his philosophical concerns is *meaningfulness*. Having faced the reality of his own mortality, he thinks about his life in larger terms. If he is to die someday, at least his life must make some significant difference in the world. It must add up to something beyond material rewards. It must not be absurd.

A forty-seven-year-old executive in a management consulting firm reflected about his life accomplishments.

By all rights I should be sitting on top of the world. My wife says we're in good shape. Lucky. Look what I've accomplished in twenty-five years. A paid-up mortgage for a three bedroom split. All ours except for taxes. A drawer in a desk with bankbooks—cash reserves, policies; cars are paid for. "In great shape." So this is what I have to show for twenty-five years. My contribution to the world. All that's missing is the gold watch. I'll get one the day I retire. A tradition around here. Twenty-five years ago I began filling "in" baskets and taking papers out of "out" baskets. Twenty-five years later it's the same thing. I think writers and artists are lucky people. Sure they might not have a paid-up mortgage, but they got something to show for their lives. Me—there's nothing. Not one thing I can lay a handle on that is meaningful. You tell someone something like this, and they think you're crazy. My wife and I used to plan and dream about being in this kind of position

—no debts, clear mortgage, retirement plans. Big deal. And it's all absurd.

This search for greater meaning is at the core of the mid-forties man's discontent with the daily routines of his life. Up to this point, he has had to be concerned about his bank balance, the mortgage, the in- and out-baskets of his work. There was sufficient challenge, excitement, and satisfaction derived from the process of "making it" in the adult world, achieving the status and rewards of success. But now there is a hollow ring to these rewards.

It is not easy, however, to break loose from an ideology that has been so much a part of his life for so many years. In addition to the stretches of grumbling and discontent, there are periods of intense anxiety, utter confusion, and occasionally even panic. At times, neither he nor the world makes any sense at all, and at such moments he may yearn for a womblike withdrawal into quiet passivity. But at this stage in his development he cannot remain quietly passive very long. He moves in one direction, then another, examining, questioning, reexamining, searching, and doubting.

Like other areas of his life, the philosophical wanderings of the mid-forties man are characterized by massive inconsistencies and sometimes daily swings from one set of beliefs to another. A radical rebel one day, an arch-conservative the next—it is not a frivolous, sophomoric game, but a symptom and a product of his serious unrest. In some ways this period of shifting ideologies is reminiscent of the earlier identity crisis, when, as a young man, he was experimenting with various belief systems. But there is a crucial difference. As a younger man, he had an underlying sense of optimism and a healthy capacity for strong belief. His ideological swings during that period were largely swings in *belief*—belief in one system and then belief in another. Now, having lived another quarter of a century, his capacity for belief has weakened, and his tendency toward disbelief has been pro-

portionately strengthened. Thus, rather than reflecting
swings in belief, his ideological shifts from day to day reflect
swings in skepticism or disbelief. It is as if he has been
psychologically "burned" by his previous acceptance of a
particular ideology, and once he begins to question his own
earlier point of view, he cannot easily accept any other. He
can no longer comfortably accept one economic scheme,
one religious creed, one point of view as the general panacea
for all the problems of his life. Thus, his fundamental difficulty is not merely the lack of a new and appropriate set of
values, but rather, a severely weakened capacity for belief
itself.

A forty-six-year-old junior college professor spoke about
his desire to regain some of the beliefs of his youth.

I think what bothers me most about my age is an
awareness that I can't believe any more. It's what I miss
most from my youth. I accept getting on in age. But
I can't face up to the doubt I feel. I can't trust any
more. I've been hurt too often. You get cheated out of
a promotion; the chairman doesn't like you, so you miss
a salary increase; you buy something in a store—like the
TV set I bought recently and it's defective and you find
you've been taken—nothing you can do. Strangers and
friends rip you off—words I've learned from my students. You knock yourself out on a course and the kids
tell you you're a failure. It's the age of student complaints. So what happens? You begin to close down and
shut out the world, and that's not what I want. I'd like
to trust, go on with naïve beliefs that people are good,
honest, fair—the government is righteous and princi-
pled, you get what you pay for—the things I believed
in as a kid, as a young man. Over the years one by one
the beliefs have been shot through, and I have nothing
to replace them with. I'm not a religious person. I
almost wish I was. Perhaps that's the appeal of religion

for some people. An enduring belief that doesn't need the world to be tested in. I'm in the world and looking for something concrete, something to give myself to, and it disturbs me that there might not be anything. My beliefs and values are on quicksand, and I'd give a lot for some firm ground.

Yet, he cannot live in a state of total skepticism. That path leads only to sour madness. He is therefore caught in the throes of an approach-avoidance conflict. He psychologically needs to believe in some ideology that will give form, meaning, and direction to his life. But the closer he gets to accepting one point of view, the greater is the strength of his skepticism. Thus, he shifts his stance from one ideology to another, never settling very long before doubt appears.

His flights from disbelief sometimes take him in strange and unpredictable directions. The Republican banker who suddenly discovers Zen Buddhism; the suburban dentist who one day finds truth, beauty, and the answers to all life's questions in vegetarianism; the stockbroker who sees the light in a back-to-the-earth commune. In each case the ideological flight is honest and sincere, but none of these flights is likely to last very long. The banker has seen too much of the world to put on the blinders necessary for a commitment to the Zen way. The dentist is much too knowledgable to find long-term fulfillment in avoiding meat. The stockbroker has experienced too much of humanity to accept for very long the bland optimism of communal living. Disbelief grows stronger, and again the ideological search begins.

late forties

Putting It Back Together

"It's a good feeling when you don't have to knock yourself out worrying about whether the whole world loves you."

The mid-forties is a time of discomfort, but it is also a time of active change. It is a time for breaking out of previous patterns, for trying new behaviors and new perspectives. Many errors are made that are embarrassing, even punishing, but some of these attempts to change are successful. They result in satisfying experiences that are gradually incorporated into an emerging new sense of self. Thus, during the difficult middle forties, there is great potential for psychological growth. And with this growth, there is movement into a new stage, the late forties, which involves a reintegration and stabilization of identity.

Every person grows at a different pace and in different directions during the period of the mid-forties. Therefore, we cannot specify the precise nature of change that occurs in each individual. Nevertheless, there are certain characteristics of growth that are more or less widely shared, and it is these general characteristics that we can consider in this stage of development.

After the stormy and sometimes painful fireworks of the mid-forties, it may be surprising to discover that the man in his late forties, at least superficially, appears to be quite similar to the kind of person he was before entering the crisis period of the decade. This apparent similarity is due to the fact that the direction of the psychological growth and change throughout the forties is congruent with the individual's earlier personality. This does not rule out the possibility of truly revolutionary changes, but in general, at every stage in human development, the direction of growth is consistent with the direction of growth established earlier in the individual's life. We do not mean that everyone's personality is rigidly determined by his early experiences. But in most instances, the ways in which a person develops are congruent with the ways in which he has developed in the past. Thus, the withdrawn introvert, though he may have bouts of extremely active social interaction during his mid-forties, usually does not become an extroverted, life-of-the-party person in his late forties. Similarly, the man who has enjoyed relatively quiet, intellectual activities throughout his earlier life does not usually give up these activities entirely to become a totally nonintellectual outdoorsman. Despite the occasionally radical trial and error, the wide swings of behavior, the dramatic shifts in attitudes shown in the middle forties, the overall trend of human development tends to be continuous. Thus, from an outside point of view, the personality of the late-forties man may look very much like his pre-forties personality.

However, even from an external perspective, though the individual's overall style of life may seem essentially the same, there are quite likely to be important changes in the *pattern* of his personality. He may, for example, show a significant change in the pattern of his interests and activities. Some aspects of his personality that were once minor may now become more important, and elements of his personality that were once predominant may become less central. The man who was at one time only conventionally, superficially religious may discover, during the trials and errors of his mid-forties, profound values in religion. The man who once viewed intellectual activities as a relatively minor part of his life may discover a new sense of fulfillment in exercising his intelligence, and become actively engaged in more intellectual pursuits. But these interests, values, and activities are not likely to be entirely foreign to his previous life; rather, they represent shifts in emphasis.

The changes in personality pattern are not random. In part, they depend upon the unique experiences encountered in the course of the trial-and-error experimentation in the middle forties. If there has been a sense of reward for changing in one direction, this particular direction of change may be reenforced.

The wife of a forty-seven-year-old vice-president of a consulting firm described her husband's enthusiastic painting efforts.

My husband never had time for hobbies. He's a twenty-four-hour-a-day man, which is hard for anyone not married to a successful person to understand. A month's vacation at our summer place for him was always torture. I dreaded it. He would sit around absolutely miserable—that is, until last summer. It's almost ridiculous what happened. We have a place on Martha's Vineyard, and I don't have to tell anyone who's been there that the place crawls with art. My husband has always made fun of these weekend artists, as he calls them. But last summer he had a birthday while we were there, and one of our friends gave him a set of oils. Now, the fact is, I know my husband was once interested in art. He'll never tell anyone, but he was a cartoonist on his high school newspaper, and in college he did the illustrations for a campus magazine. We have all the copies in the basement of our Connecticut place.

He started fooling around with the oils. I know it was desperation. We had three more weeks, and I wondered how we were going to get through them. He went down to the wharf one day and began painting, and it was really funny because he put on a beret and scarf and was really making a joke, but when he got home he told me a ludicrous story. Some tourists had come over, people out for the day, and the woman asked him if he were an artist, and he said yes, and she asked him if she could buy his picture when he finished. She wanted to give him ten dollars. It was a good picture. I was really surprised because he hadn't painted in years. He has a rather nice touch. Of course, he wouldn't take her money. I wanted the picture.

He did some more, and at a benefit one of our clubs was having one of his pictures brought in the biggest amount of money. All of us in the family were floored. I had a budding artist on my hands. He didn't want to leave at the end of the month, and we stayed for an extra few weeks, and I think he did a canvas a day. For fifteen years I've gone out of my mind trying to get him into some kind of diversion. That summer I couldn't get him away from his easel. We had the whole house littered with linseed oil, palettes, canvases, brushes in all my kitchen glasses. He hasn't stopped since. He continued after we came home. I told him watch out or the business will go and we can't eat the paintings. He half-jokingly told me he's given serious thought to selling out and spending full time as a painter. He's good, but not that good. I'd much prefer it stayed as a hobby. He's been selling his work. Three paintings this fall and one of the art stores in town told him whenever he's ready they'll give him a one-man show.

But the changes that occur are not merely a product of external rewards and reenforcements. To a large extent, they also reflect elements of the individual's personality that have been latent, perhaps inhibited during the busy years of career building, and now gain an opportunity for overt expression. A systems analyst in his mid-forties talked about how much he enjoyed writing poetry when he was an adolescent, but in resolving his earlier identity crisis, he came to see himself as a hard-headed, practical businessman who couldn't afford to waste time on trivialities such as poetry. As a consequence of this self-concept, during the years in which he was working his way up the ladder of business success, he inhibited any impulse even to read, much less write, poetry. These kinds of activities didn't fit in with the more general ways in which he saw himself, and any poetic interest he had remained latent for more than two decades. In fact, he had forgotten about his earlier poetry-writing efforts.

But during the stress of his early- and mid-forties crisis, his inhibitions weakened, and previously dormant impulses were expressed as part of his trial-and-error behavior. He began to write some poetry—at first just jotting down a line or two during moments of reflection. Then, later, finding the experience pleasurable, resonating with some hidden part of himself, he began to write more systematically, devoting substantial periods of time to his writing, gradually becoming more skillful and feeling a sense of pride and intrinsic satisfaction in his creative efforts. As a result of these experiences, this aspect of himself became increasingly important, and when he began to be engaged in a reintegration of his identity in the late forties, his once-latent interest in poetry became an important, consciously recognized and valued part of himself. In this sense, then, there was a restructuring of his personality.

Although the reintegrated identity of the late-forties man derives, in part, from the learning and reenforcement of specific behaviors, far more important is the fundamental shift in the way he sees, understands, and values himself and the world. It is this ideology which provides a basic framework for his experience and behavior; therefore, it is crucial to understand the process of reintegrating his ideology.

Underlying the breakdown in the ideological stance of the

man in his early forties was his feeling that the ways he understood himself and the world no longer made sense in terms of his current everyday experience. As a result, the perspective from which he perceived and experienced his life was shaken.

The resulting crisis led him into a period of active search for another point of view, and throughout this stage of development he struggled with conflicts of belief versus disbelief. It is this struggle that provides the dynamic force for reintegration of his ideology in the late forties.

As a consequence of his discomfort and dissatisfaction, the man in his middle forties withdraws somewhat from activities and the pursuit of goals that have occupied him for nearly a quarter of a century. This process of withdrawal provides him with an opportunity to view himself and his everyday world from a psychological distance that up to this point has been impossible to achieve. He has been thoroughly immersed in the daily routines and challenges of his life, and he has focused on immediate problems, particular tasks. Thus, he experienced life from the perspective of total immersion in the concrete realities of building a career, raising a family, fulfilling the goals of an identity he had established as a young adult. Without this immersion, he probably could not have accomplished what was necessary in his twenties and thirties. He couldn't psychologically afford to maintain a reflective, philosophical view of himself and his world—there was too much to do and he was too busy doing it.

The price that the twenty- and thirty-year-old pays for this immersion is, of course, a loss of distance in his view of life, and in terms of his needs during early adulthood, this price is well worth paying. But with the crisis of the forties and the resultant psychological withdrawal from the immediacies of everyday life, the perspective changes. The man in his middle forties stands back to gain a new view of himself in his world. He no longer sees himself simply as a business executive working his way to the top of the company, or a physician striving to gain greater technical competence and a larger practice, or a salesman engaged in the race of setting bigger and bigger sales records. Instead, he may see his world from many different perspectives—as artist, philosopher, lover, poet, athlete, scholar, economist, father, son—the possibilities are virtually endless. He may for a time see the world as a photographer does, intrigued with forms, colors, the aesthetic meanings of experience. He then shifts, sees the world another way, but his brief life from the perspective of a photographer leaves its mark. He can no longer see the world only from the viewpoint of business executive, physician, salesman. Aspects of the photographer's vision remain, perhaps no longer central, but nevertheless coloring, influencing the ways he experiences his world. He may not remain with any single point of view very long, but each experiment leaves some residual effect—and it is this residual effect that is crucially important in determining the overall direction of his ideological development.

A forty-nine-year-old marketing executive viewed his hobby as having had a significant influence on his view of life.

I got on to this photography kick through chance. I used to think these people with cameras slung over their shoulders were nuts. They never looked at the world except through a camera lens. I could eat my words. I'm as bad as the worst of them. But, you know, I really feel that photography has been different for me. It's not just a record of what I see. I go on a trip, and I like to play around with the scenes, getting the angle and lighting the way I want. It's hard to put in words, but it's a new dimension of the world—an extra look in on the world. I look at someone's face now. I think, O.K., a photograph would give me a record of the face, but I want more than that—just an angle here or a shadow and the whole perspective is changed. I'm so hooked on it that even when I'm not thinking about photography I approach a problem the same way—the off angle, the extra dimension, the extra touch. With me it's not the equipment or the doing that counts. I see photography not only as a hobby but just a special way of seeing the world.

As he moves from the middle forties into the late forties, the rhythm of his changing perspectives slows down, and the direction of change becomes more clearly focused. He goes from a stage of generalized disbelief, which is humanly impossible to maintain over a long period of time, to a stage in which he allows himself the comforts of belief for longer, then somewhat longer, and even longer periods of time. It is not easy to shake loose from his impulse to disbelieve, but his need to have some more or less consistent framework within which to make sense of his life is far stronger than any acquired cynicism. And gradually, he comes to find greater significance and satisfaction in one or another ideological direction. Like other aspects of his personality growth during this period, the resultant, reintegrated ideology is significantly different from that with which he began the decade, but the change is also congruent with his past. In almost all instances, the ideologies of the early and late forties are members of the same family—one might say siblings derived from the same basic stock.

If we compare the point of view of the man in his late forties with that of the man at the onset of this decade of crisis, there are two interrelated characteristics of development that stand out. In the late forties, his view of his life and his world is both more clearly differentiated and better integrated. One might think of a person's ideological framework as a kind of jigsaw puzzle. In the early forties, the distinctions between one part of the puzzle and another may be somewhat blurred, and the interrelationships among the various parts may be unclear and overlapping. In the mid-forties, the puzzle is thoroughly shaken up, and pieces fall in many different directions. But then in the late forties the process of reintegration begins. Each part of the puzzle comes to be more clearly distinguished, and the ways in which the various parts fit in with one another are more firmly defined. Throughout these years the pieces of the puzzle remain essentially the same, but as the end of the decade approaches, the way in which each part fits into the whole pattern becomes clearer and better organized.

This metaphor of ideological development can be translated back into the terms of life during the forties. During the early and middle forties, work and family life often overlap and may interfere with each other. But the late-forties perspective permits a clearer distinction of one part of life from another, and a fuller appreciation of the relationships between these parts. Thus, work and family life are more sharply differentiated—and at the same time better integrated. He no longer brings home the dozens of problems he encounters daily in his work. He can temporarily set them aside while he enjoys family life. In addition, he can distinguish between the problems of these two realms of experience. At one time, frustrations in work would have led to tension at home, and problems in his family life would have disturbed him in his work. But now he can appreciate the boundaries between these two areas of his life. It would be unreasonable to assume that he now leads a tension-free existence on the job. But he can view his work problems from a more distant perspective, and they are much less likely to flood over into other aspects of his life. Similarly, he can better distinguish the goals, motives, satisfactions of work from those of family life. He may recognize that he can express his motivations for power and mastery primarily in his job, and he need not play the role of "boss" or "foreman" in his home. Conversely, he is more likely to understand that he can satisfy much of his need for affection within his family, and he no longer feels driven to seek this affection from those with whom he works.

A forty-nine-year-old sales executive commented on his reactions to acceptance or rejection in his relationships with other people.

It used to count with me what the other guy thought. I wanted to make an impression—be liked. Sure, if you're a salesman, as I started out, a lot counts if you're liked. I was the kind of guy who couldn't even walk into a restaurant and have the head waiter approach me without worrying if he liked me. Neurotic—O.K., neurotic. What other people thought counted on my scoreboard. I don't give a damn any more. I don't go out of my way to hurt other people, but I sure as hell face up to the fact that some people like you and some don't. There's not much you can do about it. I give a square deal, and if the guys I got working under me don't like it, the hell with them. I'm not out to get anyone and I'm not out to make anyone crawl at my feet. I got myself to worry about. There's one life that counts— mine. I'm not crawling any more. I don't want anyone crawling to me. It's a good feeling when you don't have to knock yourself out worrying about whether the whole world loves you.

We have discussed the ideological reintegration of the late forties as an ideal goal. Obviously, it is not always accomplished smoothly and perfectly. Reintegration is a matter of degree, rather than an all-or-none, absolute state. Moreover, this reintegration is a process that goes on over time as the late-forties man gradually grows, changes, and achieves a more harmonious and satisfying reintegration of himself and his life.

Balancing Freedom and Need

*"I seem now to be riding strong in the best of
both—my freedom . . . my family."*

No area of existence is more frequently or dramatically disrupted for the mid-forties man than his marital and family
life. Sometimes the bonds developed over the previous years
are so strained by the crisis of the forties that the marriage
relationship is broken. Divorce ensues—and with remarkable frequency, the middle-forties man remarries. In any
event, regardless of whether we consider a marriage that has
withstood the stresses of the forties or a new marriage that
is, in part, a consequence of these stresses, the relationships
of the man in his late forties with his wife and family are
somewhat different from the past. One of the most striking
differences is an increasing sense of his independence and
a parallel awareness as well as acceptance of his dependency.

A forty-eight-year-old business manager discusses the
changes in his attitudes toward family life.

Thinking back, there were times we were on shaky
ground. I was pressured from my job and my family. I
couldn't keep them straight. I had the feeling it was
one or the other—had to be. I'm lucky about my wife.
She had to put up with a lot. The trips I had to take,
moves we made, new houses, new friends, the kids—
it was rough going, and I guess I wasn't much of a help.
I told her I've reached a point in life when I can have
both—I need both. I need my job, my position. I've
worked too hard and too long to give it all up. On the
other hand, I need her and the kids. It's something I
really count on at the end of a day. We do a lot together
—more than we ever did before. I'm not trying to make
up for lost time. You don't do that. But it's nice to

realize for me that I seem now to be riding strong in the best of both—my freedom and my wanting what lots of people, I suppose, call family chains. If that's what they are called by some people, here's one person who wants the lock put on and the key thrown away.

A forty-nine-year-old regional manager for a manufacturer of hard goods talked about the difference between his first and second marriage.

My first marriage was a farce. My former wife accused me of not wanting to give myself to a family. She blamed me for what went wrong, said I wasn't prepared to give up anything for her or the kids. Sure I wanted independence, but that isn't the whole story by a long shot. I take a good long look at the way my present marriage has worked out. My wife and I have a child. I don't complain about helping her. Many a night I've been up with the baby, and when you're forty-nine let me tell you it isn't pure joy to get up for a four o'clock bottle. But I figure she has the whole day she has to take care of him, so I can pitch in. What difference does it make except a few hours less sleep? That's what I mean. In this marriage I am independent, but I also need my wife—the baby—being there. They're very important in my life. It's a balance—it isn't what I had in my first marriage. They wanted everything of me, wanted to keep me tied down. For my own sanity I had to get out. She never understood how I felt. This time around I told my present wife, "There are times each of us has to be ourselves, and there are other times we sure as hell need each other."

In the course of his troubled experimentation, the mid-forties man often resented his own feelings of dependency on others as much as he resented their dependence on him.

As a result, he frequently struck out, sometimes explosively for total freedom, as he saw it, from the chains that bound him to the previous patterns of his life. It was a matter of being either totally independent or totally dependent, with no viable middle ground between. And for the most part, he consciously strove to move in the direction of independence.

Yet, no person can live a totally independent life, just as no person can live very long in a state of total disbelief. Particularly at times of psychological stress, despite his vigorous conscious efforts to gain total freedom, the man in his middle forties needed others perhaps more than at any other time in his adult life. He needed their psychological support, their reassurance, their sympathetic understanding and acceptance. His drive to gain a sense of autonomy represented honest, sincere motivation, and it was an important part of his development. But at the same time, he also needed to depend upon others. Thus, he was caught in a dilemma, and the violent swings in his behavior partly reflected this dilemma. He might have aggressively rejected any feelings of dependency on his wife, but then become involved in an exceedingly dependent extramarital relationship. Or even within his marriage, he might at one moment have acted as if he wished to be totally free, and a short time later behaved in an utterly dependent way.

The wife of a supermarket manager in his middle forties reacted to the contradictions in her husband's behavior.

We had a big fight. He wants to go off on a fishing trip with some of his friends. Me, I'm to stay home with the kids while he goes hopping off for a week on his own. When do I ever take a vacation like that? O.K., he goes. I couldn't stop him. He doesn't need us; we don't need him. The kids and I had a great week. He comes home with a cold like you never saw. He told me he got caught in the rain and their clothes got wet. He was sick as a dog. And then he expects me to wait on him hand and foot. I get a cold, and I walk around. He gets a cold and he's up in bed moaning like he was dying. I told him take three aspirin and get back to work. He stays in bed for three days, so out of the two weeks vacation he had one wet miserable week and three days in bed. Good for him. My girl friends and I were laughing because it served the boys right—they caught colds instead of fish.

As the middle-forties man grows into his late forties, these swings of behavior become less extreme. His ideological framework is gradually reintegrated, and he gains a firmer, more confident perspective. He feels less threatened by those who are close to him, and thus his irrational strivings for total independence are considerably modified. He is no longer afraid of being completely overwhelmed by the demands of others, and he no longer needs to fight for complete freedom. As he gains a more differentiated and integrated view of himself and others, he gradually develops a surer sense of his own true autonomy.

A forty-eight-year-old office manager commented on his recent rebellion against conformity.

We live in a neighborhood where everyone acts like a carbon copy. For years it's been that way; paint the house every two years, keep the crab grass off the lawn. Sure, no one comes out directly and tells you what to do, but the feeling is there; you hear about it in small ways; my wife hears about it; someone makes a remark to the kids. It's the same, I suppose, everywhere in a house, an apartment, but I had enough. This year I told my wife I'm not going to mow the grass every week. I'll do things around the house when I want to. It's the same with a lot of things. I don't have to put white trim on my house just because everyone on the street has white trim. I'll put on purple if I want to. I told my kids we'd join the town swim club if we wanted to, and not because everyone else is joining.

Somewhere along the line of life you have to come to grips with yourself. You do what you want to because you feel that way; you don't have to follow the rules. I'm not out to stir up a revolution by a long shot. I just want to be my own self. If I feel like wearing a tie and jacket I'll wear one, not because everyone else has one on. We don't have to trade in an old car unless we want to. I'm sick of these kind of pressures, and I feel for the first time in my life that I don't need to jump through hoops just because friends and neighbors nod their heads and say "jump."

Meanwhile, he has also experienced the very real rewards of dependency. When he was battling against depression, his feelings of defeat and worthlessness, he was likely to have received some degree of psychological support and reassurance from others—from his wife or someone outside of his immediate family. And when he moved in one direction and then another during his period of trial and error, if he was fortunate, he probably experienced some acceptance, maybe even encouragement, and at least the partial understanding of another person. Despite the fights, the hostility, the pain, there is almost always a thread of interpersonal support, and it is precisely because of the emotional intensity of the mid-forties crisis that this support acquires greater value. In a sense, it was actually the process of living through the crisis itself that provided an opportunity to recognize and appreciate the inevitability and the positive value of human interdependence.

A fifty-year-old businessman discussed his feelings about his family's support during a crisis.

One experience taught me a lesson I won't forget. I told my family maybe some good came out of the bad.

I learned who was behind me. Recession shot the hell out of my business. I had some bad luck, whatever, I hit bottom. It was rough going. I lost everything; it's the way the deals landed. One way a big success, the other nothing. Very bad for the kids, for me, my wife. We sold the house, everything we had. It isn't easy when you have kids my kids' ages to pull back like that. One day they had pocket money, and the next I am borrowing from their savings. What do you do? We were stuck. My wife said nothing. She took a job as a bookkeeper. Not one word from anyone. I'm sitting holding my head, crying like hell inside, and the rest of them are knocking themselves out. I tell you, they pulled me through a rough time.

In one year I was back on my feet. Sure, we aren't on top yet, but things are fine. They wouldn't let me drown. I told my wife later, she wouldn't even cry on my shoulder. She said she'd be damned she'd cry because we lost everything. That's how she took it. I think it made us all stronger as a family. Take my son, I was always giving him advice. One day when I was trying to decide whether to plunge again I asked him what I should do. He came across. I told them all how I felt. I told them, "Look, I have a temper; I make mistakes. But, remember, no matter what, they better not forget that inside the family counts."

These two strands of development, the experience of greater autonomy as well as honest and rewarding dependency, join together as the man in his late forties reintegrates his identity. By virtue of experiencing both his growing sense of autonomy and his real dependency, he comes to accept the fact that independence and dependence are not necessarily contradictory or incompatible. In fact, they are complementary aspects of any mature, close interpersonal relationship.

This realization has profound implications for his marriage (or remarriage, as the case may be). His feelings of being threatened by his wife decrease, and the stormy fights about seemingly trivial issues become less and less frequent. Because he feels more confidently autonomous, he can afford to express more openly his affection and his need for another person. He and his wife have lived through the problems of the forties together, and if their marriage has withstood the stresses and strains, they have, as a result, probably grown closer together. The late forties can be a period of married life that is psychologically more intimate than ever before.

The wife of a forty-nine-year-old C.P.A. talked about a recent closeness between her and her husband.

I was at my husband's office last week, and his secretary told me that my husband was the first boss she had who dropped everything when his wife called. She thought it was wonderful that I came up once, sometimes twice a week for lunch if I was in the area.

I wouldn't tell her that it hasn't always been this way. The last years we've been through plenty of trouble. He was running all the time, running from me, the children, the house, the family. My mother always said you don't know what goes on behind closed doors. She was right. We had one face for the world and another face for in the house. Nothing was going right. If I said blue, he'd say yellow; if I said red, he'd say white. It was just about that level. I think his unhappiness was a combination of a lot of things—business, problems with the children. Many a time I said to myself, Leave him. But I didn't want that. So I waited, and I'm glad now because we've been closer now than ever before. I don't mean just doing things. Lunch together isn't it—we talk together, and we can really understand each other.

An interesting, if somewhat surprising, phenomenon often occurs at this stage of development. The late-forties husband frequently acts as if he has completely forgotten the battles through which he and his wife so recently lived. If pushed, he can of course recall some of the more dramatic events of this time, but their emotional strength seems to have been lost. If he has remained married throughout this period, this apparent "forgetting" may at first be disconcerting to his wife. As the prime target of much of his hostility, she is not likely to forget the pain of these experiences so readily. If he has been divorced and remarried, his new wife is unlikely to be aware of the extraordinary emotional intensity of these earlier conflicts. She knows, of course, that he was unhappy and dissatisfied in his previous marriage, but she does not associate the affectionate, understanding, mellowed man she has married with the highly emotional, conflicted, and occasionally very hostile person he once was.

The forty-eight-year-old wife of a cardiac surgeon talked about her last few years of marriage and the struggles to remain together.

My husband and I recently took a vacation—the first we've taken together in about four years. It was perfect. I felt much like I did when we were first married—wanted, appreciated, loved. Just the two of us. We didn't know anyone, nor did we try and get to know anyone at the resort. My husband insisted he wanted to be alone with me. I was all he wanted. One evening I happened to mention to him it was the first time we'd been alone like this and feeling good about it for years. He insisted it wasn't true—that we always took vacations together. He forgot, completely forgot or repressed, I don't know which, what happened to us all those years. I wanted to ask him about that "other woman" I knew he had an affair with. I would love to find out about those weekends when he supposedly was

at conferences, and I knew there weren't any conferences because I asked around and found out the truth.
  He told me I had changed, more like I was when we
first were married. Perhaps I have. I don't think so. I
think he's the one who has changed. There's no point
in reminding him of the nights I sat up waiting, the
hysterics I had with the door closed to keep the children from hearing. For me a set of tiring, bad memories
—for him just the far past and the present. I'll keep it
all to myself. It is strange though because, if what he
says and the way he behaves are true, there's no doubt
in my mind that it's all been blotted out. Every scene,
every show of temper, every heartache I endured have
been forgotten.

A young operating-room nurse recently married to a forty-
nine-year-old neurosurgeon noted the contrast between her
marriage and stories she hears about her husband's first
marital experience.

I'm always having someone throw in a dig about my
husband and how I can stand his temper. Honestly, I
don't know what they're talking about. One of the gals
at work, a supervisor, once told me that she had heard
how my husband was impossible with his first wife. She
knew some doctor who lived out near where he did, and
I guess everyone talked about the family battles. I hate
this kind of gossip. Another friend of mine who had
once been at a cocktail party with my husband when
he was still married to his first wife told me there had
been a terrible scene. Evidently his wife insulted him
in front of the whole hospital staff. I wasn't working
here then. In fact, I only met him when he was getting
a divorce, and we didn't start dating right away anyhow. I mean, I wasn't involved in that first marriage
trouble.

If he had a temper or if I even suspected he had a temper, forget it. I'm rather easygoing, and I wouldn't put up with any guy who blew his top—say if I met him for dinner and I was late. With me my husband is a doll. I've seen him at work and at the apartment, and he's no different—calm, cool, and underneath a big soft baby. He can't do enough for me. Last week it was a riot—I had the flu and he decided to play nurse, so he makes breakfast and brings in this soft-boiled egg I couldn't cut with a knife! Patients here are lucky he's a surgeon and not a nurse. People misread each other. I've found that out. Sometimes he's got to put on a front but believe you me underneath he's as gentle and soft . . . a real honey.

Having gone through periods of feast and famine during his early- and mid-forties, the late-forties male finds that his sexual life returns to a pattern more similar to the pre-forties. However, this part of his life has been enlivened and enriched by his opportunities for learning during the recent stage of experimentation. As a result, his repertoire of sexual behaviors has expanded, his inhibitions have been somewhat loosened, and having experienced episodes of intense sexual arousal and activity, the fears of losing his virility are greatly reduced. Thus, the late forties can be a new stage of sexual maturity, often characterized by an attitude of relaxed enjoyment, a sense of sureness and expertise, and a deeper capacity both to give and receive pleasure.

A forty-nine-year-old owner of an import-export firm commented about the role of sex in his current life.

When I was a kid if my folks had heard the word sex mentioned in the house my mother would have had a heart attack and my father the same. I certainly never associated my parents with sex. Sex was for other people—not for my mother and dad. None of us kids

talked about sex in relation to our parents. It was embarrassing to even think that any of us were conceived
through sex. You didn't think about it and certainly
never talked about it. Things have changed. My own
kid asked me, "At your age do you still enjoy sex?" I
was thrown for a loop. I'm not fifty yet, and he has me
out of commission. He should only know. I don't find
it easy talking sex with him. It's a hangup talking about
it with my own kids.

As far as enjoying myself, let me tell you it's never
been better. I told my wife all those years I was knocking myself out in business I was missing some great
times. I told her we got a lot to make up for. I'm pretty
lucky from what I gather because my wife and I see it
the same way. As far as we're concerned, we're not
going to waste the next years, you better believe me.
It's about the *only* thing in life I've decided you can
do over and over, and the next time is just as good or
even better than the last.

It would be unreasonable to assume that long-term, deep-
seated sexual problems are automatically resolved at this
stage. But to a large extent, the normal fears and anxieties
concerning developmental sexual problems are significantly
decreased. By his late forties, he no longer interprets the
natural physical consequence of fatigue as a sign of lost
virility, and he no longer views temporarily reduced sexual
drive as a threat to his manhood. He can more realistically
differentiate sexuality from masculinity, power, aggression,
and he can better integrate this important aspect of his life
with other areas of living. Sex is no longer experienced as a
test of his psychological and physical potency; rather, in the
late forties, it becomes a significant part of an interpersonal
relationship. Now a man's sexual behavior reflects the twin
themes of autonomy and dependence, in that he engages in
sex as an independent, mature adult who also recognizes and

appreciates his fundamental interdependence with his partner.

If the turbulence of the early- and mid-forties was severe enough to lead to divorce, for a while, the mid-forties man may have led a bachelor existence. But by his late forties, he is often remarried—sometimes to a person with whom he has had an extramarital relationship.

Like other aspects of his life, his new marriage may seem, at least on the surface, to be quite similar to his previous marriage. Casual acquaintances may wonder why he went through the trouble of dissolving one marriage only to begin another one that is so much the same. But beyond the superficial similarities, the second relationship is likely to be quite different from the first.

The new marriage, of course, begins at quite a different stage of life. The man in his late forties has changed significantly in ways that are important for marriage. Obviously, the external conditions are quite different from those under which he began his earlier marriage. He is established in his career, has a fairly good idea of what he can reasonably hope to achieve in his work. More important than the external conditions, however, are the internal changes. He has a clearer sense of his own tastes, values, goals. He has a better-integrated view of himself and his world. Perhaps most important—as we have discussed in the area of sexual activities—he has a firmer sense of his own autonomy, as well as a fuller appreciation of his need for others. Thus, he is much less prone to being caught in a conflict between irrational strivings for independence and neurotic impulses toward dependency. In many important respects, therefore, he is a better candidate for successful marriage in his late forties than ever before. This is true both in a continuing marriage and in a new one.

Remarriages are by no means the panacea for all the psychological problems of the forties, but neither are they especially susceptible to troubles. Like any other close human relationship, they involve a degree of risk, a degree of stress, and some potential for success. Among those who are living through the trials and errors of the middle forties, there are some who are convinced that the perfect solution to all of their problems is divorce and remarriage. There are others who are equally convinced that divorce is an absolute sign of personal failure and that any remarriage is bound to fail. Neither point of view provides the whole answer. In dealing with the developmental problems of the forties—as with any psychological problems—there is no simple prescription that is valid for everyone.

Power Without Ego

"I don't have to sit around telling everyone at the bar how good I am, and I don't care how good they are."

In his late forties a man often shows a renewed interest in his work, but without some of the intensity that characterized his earlier striving. Given the shift in the ideological perspective from which he sees himself and his world, he seeks somewhat different values in his career. He is likely to have reconciled himself to a more realistic level of achievement, and while he is still ambitious and achievement-oriented, his goals are usually tempered by considerations other than the acquisition of money and power.

In the actual world of his work, he may have more power than ever before. Yet, he often is less concerned with power than he was when he was striving to gain it. There are, of course, dictatorial authoritarians among the ranks of late-forties men, just as there are at any age, but by and large, the late forties is not a time in which the drive for power is a primary motivating force. As a matter of fact, the meaning of power often changes at this stage. Earlier in life, power was seen primarily in terms of the capacity to influence others and to be free from external control. But now this view is modified by a new dimension: The man in his late forties is likely to experience his position of power largely in terms of the responsibilities associated with it.

The forty-nine-year-old president of a junior college talked about his attitudes toward his position.

When you're on the outside looking in, you have the notion that the person on top views his position as one of power. I remember years ago when I first came on the faculty as an instructor beginning to move up the ladder, I felt that way about the chairman of the department, the top people in administration. They had power, and power alone motivated them. I wanted power, I admit, because I too wanted my ideas gotten across. Since I took over the presidency, the whole notion of power just isn't there. The job has turned out to be one of responsibilities, headaches, constant problems I never can avoid. Yes, there's power in the role, but it's overshadowed by the very real work involved of being responsible to the job, to the people under you, and to yourself. I can remember the day after I was in this office I realized this fact. The novelty wore off in one day with me. The real truth is that alone in this office you've got the whole ladder of people out there, the faculty, students, secretaries, and even the maintenance people to worry about.

If the slackening of the drive for power as an ego-enhancer affects the attitude toward work in the late forties, there is a comparable shift in the function of play. Recreational activities usually become less emotionally intensive than they were in the middle forties, and also more narrowly focused. While the mid-forties man may engage in a wide variety of activities, by the late forties he is much more selective, concentrating his play in the one or two areas which he has found most satisfying.

Enjoyment of the activity for its own sake becomes a major theme. This is in marked contrast to the middle-forties man, for whom play has all kinds of *extra* meanings other than enjoyment. As we have seen, play may represent an opportunity to express his masculinity, a chance to demonstrate his "youthful" strength and energy, a means of trying out various aspects of his emerging identity. But by the late forties, these meanings become far less important than the intrinsic pleasure of the activity itself. In this sense, the man in his late forties is much more of a simple hedonist. He doesn't play to build up his body or show that he is still youthful; he doesn't play to satisfy his needs for power or impress others with his ability. By and large, he plays just for the fun of it.

A forty-seven-year-old bank officer reacted to his change in attitude toward his golf score.

The club is having a tournament, and one of the guys asked me why I wasn't entering. I told him I don't need an ego trip trophy. He told me I could walk away with it. I can do without the gold plate on a bookshelf. I know I used to feel differently. Five years ago I would have been the first to sign up for a tournament. In fact, I probably would have organized it. Now, what's the difference? I play to relax, not to win. I was out last week with one of the guys, and I told myself, "Never again." I don't need a Saturday afternoon hassel over scores. Sure I like to play well. A low score gives me satisfaction, but I don't have to sit around telling everyone at the bar how good I am, and I don't care how good they are. Golf is a way for me to unwind from pressures, a pleasant afternoon on a good day. I don't need dust-collecting trophies in the basement.

The forties begin at a peak of energy, ambition, and activity. The emotional tone of life then drops sharply into a period of melancholy and doubt. This leads to a stage of experimentation, trial and error, a time when life is often confusing and contradictory. But then, after the stresses of these years, the promise of psychological growth in the forties is realized. There is a reintegration of identity, a clearer view of oneself and the world, and a deeper appreciation of the positive values of one's life. Having negotiated the crisis of this decade, the man in his late forties can look forward to his fifties, a period of relative psychological tranquility— a time when he can recoup his psychic energies and enjoy the satisfactions of his maturity.

The wife of a lawyer described a recent party she gave in honor of her husband's fiftieth birthday.

I went through pure hell before deciding to go ahead. I had no idea how he would react. Knowing him, I expected a scene. He's always been difficult about parties in his honor. I think it has something to do with the way he was brought up. He's told me as a kid his mother never did anything for his birthdays. Well, whatever, I made the decision and expected the worst. I can't tell you what a dream it all turned out to be. I had gone all out with a caterer—the whole bit.

And the people I invited. It was like an old TV show —people from the past dragged out of nowhere. Some old army buddies he hadn't seen in years; his high school sweetheart—yes, I found her married name and traced her down. I'm not kidding, though, when I say that sometimes during the planning I got cold feet and thought I must be mad to gamble on his reactions the way I was doing. It could have been a disaster. Don't think it didn't cross my mind that he would walk in and walk out and leave me standing there with all those guests.

People were told to park as far as they could from the house. I knew if he had any hint of a party when he came home he would get right back in his car and disappear. I couldn't take any chances. All I told him was that maybe we would go out to dinner if he liked, and it was up to him. He said, "Fine." Why didn't I meet him at the office. Well, I made up some story, and he said he would come back and get me.

It was a beautiful evening. He walked in and no one was there. I had the people hiding out on the patio and downstairs. I was dressed, and he said, well, since I was all dressed up he'd change. He had bought himself a whole outfit recently. And then the party just went wild. People came crawling out of the corners. I was scared there for a moment, but he was marvelous. He kept going up to people and hugging them. His old high school sweetheart gave him a huge kiss. I tell you it was a riot because she was really cute about it all— she had been a cheerleader and led everyone in a cheer. It couldn't have been better.

At midnight the cake was cut and I served champagne. Everyone was standing around. I put only one candle on the cake, and he proposed a toast. He held up his glass and just stood there looking at me and at everyone and then he said, "I made a wish, and I'd like to tell everyone my wish. I hope the next years bring my wife and me as much happiness as the past years we've had together. Thanks for coming. I'm really touched." Imagine him saying that! I just stood there, and I think I started to cry because he came over and put his arm around me. He truly had forgotten everything. The past years were blacked out of his mind. Every word; every fight; I felt drained.

It flashed through my mind that it was kind of nice not being the old nagging bitch of a few years ago. Neither of us, I guess, were angels, but it had been rough going there for a while. But, you know, it's strange . . . I had this odd feeling that being fifty had its glorious rewards. We were finally adults. It had taken a long time, I suppose, and yet right then I felt we weren't old, though frankly fifty is a milestone. I felt we were both of us terribly young and grown up, all at the same time.

My daughter came over and asked if I felt relieved. She knew how worried I had been about his behavior. I told her I was dumfounded. And you know what she said to me? She said she felt guilty not reassuring me. It turns out she had let him in on all the plans. That's why he had a new outfit. The two of them had gone shopping. I remember now his buying the clothes and then just letting them hang in the closet. I had even once said to him, "Why aren't you putting on your new jacket?" He had known all along. And now it dawns on me . . . when I had been trying to find out the name of his high school sweetheart, he was the one who remembered her married name.

part three

HER

early forties

Apprehension

"It just hit me—waves of depression, all because I was turning forty."

The thirty-nine-year-old woman becomes forty with a mixture of emotions. She feels a certain sense of satisfaction in having negotiated the occasionally bumpy thirties, and she is more confident of herself in meeting everyday problems of living. She knows her own strengths and weaknesses; she feels wiser, more self-assured and poised.

These positive feelings are often counterbalanced by an underlying sense of apprehensiveness and tension, a vague discomfort, and at times a feeling of embarrassment. She may even feel ashamed of being forty. There is usually no specific external factor that accounts for these feelings; her daily life remains relatively unchanged. Her emotional reactions are based only on knowing that she is now forty years old. This awareness alone, however, may lead to a characteristic but minor crisis of aging that reflects cultural values rather than any of the specific physical changes associated with this time of life.

To understand this crisis, we must first recognize that aging is both a physical and a sociopsychological phenomenon. Physically, everyone ages from the moment life begins. It is a more or less continuous process, with gradual changes throughout the life span. Some stages are defined by the appearance of a particular kind of behavior. The development of speech, for instance, signifies a move from infancy to early childhood. Other new phases are marked by the introduction of certain activities. Beginning school, for example, indicates the end of one stage of childhood and the start of another.

Many critical points in the sociopsychological process of aging, however, are not associated with any external events. They are tied to the chronological age itself, and are as real and significant as any observable physical change in human development. It is almost as if at a given stage, between these points, the aging process stands still. For example, thirty-three is psychologically and socially no older than thirty-two; similarly, there is little or no difference between the ages of thirty-three and thirty-four.

However, at certain critical points, there may be enormous social and psychological differences between two consecutive ages. Although thirty-four is practically the same age psychologically as thirty-three, in our culture, especially for women, forty is viewed as dramatically different from thirty-nine. No physical or situational event initiates the change at forty; nonetheless, there is a clear and decisive shift in the perspective of the individual herself and the way others view her. She is no longer a "young adult," fresh, light-hearted, buoyant. She is now experienced, settled. She finds it more difficult to identify with youth and youthfulness; she is concerned that she may be "over the hill," a woman approaching matronly middle age.

There is no right or wrong in this shift to maturity, and there is certainly nothing absolute about the age of forty defining the end of young adulthood. In various cultures at various times, other ages have marked the beginning of maturity. Nevertheless, for an American woman in the twentieth century, the change from thirty-nine to forty represents a sociopsychological leap in the process of aging, and the reality of this leap is an undeniably important experience in her life. She has grown up in a culture with a particular view of the aging process, and as a member of that culture she has learned to see life within the temporal framework of her society. Very early in childhood she learned to identify and label herself and others on the basis of age roles. At first, the distinctions were quite gross. There were merely children and adults. Then, as she grew older, her discriminations became increasingly refined: babies, children, adolescents, young adults, etc. Gradually she learned to view the entire life span from the perspective of her culture's framework.

This framework involves much more than chronological definitions of life stages. It includes certain roles or expectations associated with each stage. Thus, babies are expected to behave in certain ways, children in other ways, and adolescents in still other ways.

Although these expectations are not explicit laws of society, they are often psychologically as compelling. We learn to accept them, to anticipate them as if they were simply the way life is—and must be. Adolescents are expected to be rebellious, striving for independence, rambunctious, and troublesome. In our society, they are expected to behave in these ways. By and large, they do, and we forget that their behavior is, in part, a result of our cultural expectations.

With this thoroughly learned set of age-role expectations the forty-year-old woman believes the expectations she associates with various stages of life are "natural." She has learned that forty is settled and mature, perhaps wiser but a bit dull, less buoyant, less flexible, and in some important respects, less attractive to others. She may still feel active, energetic, adventurous, but she is convinced that these feelings will pass, that she will soon be sliding unhappily toward middle age.

Although no external events initiated her changing perspective, events take on new meaning. Because she believes forty is the end of youthfulness, she will interpret physical changes, events at home and at work, almost anything that happens to her, in terms of her own aging. This does not mean that conflict is inevitable; she may be psychologically ready, even eager, to assume the age role of the forties. But in most instances, this change in perspective, this shift from young adulthood to maturity and approaching middle age is met with some reluctance and fear.

Fat and Forty

"Facing your figure when you are my age is a nightmare."

In the normal course of chronological aging, there is typically an increase in body weight. Although there are people who maintain essentially the same body weight throughout adult life, some gain in weight is so common in our culture that it may be considered, at least statistically, a normal phenomenon. Among women, this process may be further complicated by the stresses imposed on the body by childbearing. Thus, by the age of forty, there is often a thickening of the waist and an increase of fatty tissue around the hips.

This physical change doesn't occur overnight. It is a process that goes on throughout adult life. However, the psychological impact of weight gain varies from one stage of development to another. At thirty-four or thirty-five, the individual may be a few pounds overweight, but at this stage the extra weight is probably not a major concern. She tries a diet occasionally, loses some weight, perhaps gains it back, but it is probably more of a minor game than a serious psychological problem. Her extra weight does concern her, for she has learned that slimness is the American way of feminine beauty. But after all, she is a young woman vigorously engaged in the active stream of life, and a few pounds one way or the other can hardly make much of a difference in the way she sees herself or in the way others see her.

At forty the psychological picture changes radically. She feels that every extra pound, every added inch is a glaring public display of her aging. Her weight becomes the focus of intense concern, a concern that is sometimes reenforced by the reactions of others.

A forty-one-year-old woman described an experience with her husband that underscored her own worries about weight.

He's always getting some digs in about my figure. I have told him people in glass houses shouldn't throw stones. He is no Adonis. I look at my daughter, and I am envious. She has the figure I had at her age. There isn't much I can do. The pounds slip on. It's a daily fight in a losing battle.

The time I really got hurt, though, was on a trip we took to the Caribbean. I starved for weeks. I was feeling good because I had gone down almost ten pounds. When we got to the hotel I went out and bought myself a bikini. I really felt great. I put it on, and my husband didn't say one word at first. Then he told me that if I wore that suit down to the beach, he would stay in the room. It didn't matter when I told him that all the women on the beach had suits like mine. He told me they could wear them and I couldn't. He said I looked like hell. He wouldn't be seen with a middle-aged woman pretending she was sleek and twenty.

I burst out crying I felt so awful. I threw away the suit. Thirty-five dollars into the wastebasket. Bathing suits can't be returned, and there wasn't anything I could do. He asked me why I hadn't tried it on in the store. I had. The saleswoman said I looked very nice. The colors were perfect. I told her to be honest with me. I didn't think I looked bad; I thought I looked rather good. It was a terrible start to our vacation.

The importance of weight for a woman in her early forties undoubtedly derives from our culture's association of slimness with attractiveness, plus her own view of herself as going downhill. The added weight, the few more inches around the middle may be an inevitable part of growing older, but inevitable or not, in the words of an assistant bank manager in her early forties, these changes can be experienced as a nightmare.

My first day in the rhythmics class was an eye-opener. If I thought I was in bad shape, I only had to look around the room and feel I was svelte by comparison. I wonder how it happens. I know all of the women huffing in, bursting out of those leotards they had us wear, once had good figures. It's a good thing they didn't have any full-length mirrors. We would all have had heart attacks. There were such gasps of agony when the instructor had us stretch and pull.

I wonder how it happens? All of us must have started out the same way, and then each year the muscles sagged, the pounds sneaked on and stayed on, and you end up with a larger size dress. Facing your figure when you are my age is a nightmare.

The theme of inevitability crops up over and over again in the comments of women in their early forties fighting the problem of weight. Underlying most of the theories explaining the increased weight is the feeling of hopelessness expressed by a forty-two-year-old woman, the mother of three children, who talked about her struggles over the past two years.

I smell food and get fat. I don't have to eat to gain weight. I breathe calories in. I don't care what a doctor says. I am probably the only person I know to whom an extra cucumber and lettuce salad means a pound over for the day. I have noticed that the last few years it's worse than ever before. It never was this bad when I was a teenager or in my twenties, or even thirties. Now I can't remember the time I tasted a piece of cake. It's gotten to the point where going out to dinner at a restaurant is no joy. It only means I don't eat; or if I eat I spend the next day fasting.

Between you and me, women's magazines have my fantasy life all wrong. They think I am dreaming of being twenty-five, skinny, lying on a beach oiled and tanned. I'll let you in on a dream of mine. I'm riding the exercycle in the basement, panting and puffing, and I shut my eyes. There I am on a back-porch swing. No bra, girdle; just a smock, and all around me are boxes and boxes of chocolate bars. I'm working my way through the boxes, piece by piece. Sometimes when I've been at the sauna at our health club or in a rhythmics class, I wonder if all of us dragging our bottoms across the gym floor are absolutely mad. If it's that much work to keep the pounds off, why fight it? Then I get scared of what I'll look like. Let's face it. I expect to spend the rest of my life eating my way through pounds of cottage cheese.

A woman in her early forties finds herself fighting what she feels is a losing battle. At one level, it is a battle against weight. At a deeper level, it is a battle against aging, the loss of physical attractiveness, and all that this loss may imply. Of course, there are many individual differences. For some, weight gain is merely a source of temporary discomfort that is forgotten, or repressed, in the course of active involvement in everyday life. For others, a few extra pounds can be traumatic. To a certain extent, a woman's reaction depends upon the degree to which her self-esteem has been derived from her sense of physical attractiveness. If her feelings of self-worth are based largely on aspects of herself other than physical characteristics, the problem of increasing weight may seem trivial. But if physical attractiveness has been a primary source of self-esteem, the threat of becoming "fat and forty" may be devastating.

In her early forties, she pursues the goal of losing weight with a new sense of determination. She has accepted the fact that she has passed forty, but is probably not resigned to being the cultural stereotype of a post-forty woman—a dumpling.

Effective dieting is hard, of course, because it means changing eating habits that have been acquired over years. But the most dedicated dieters in the world are probably women in their early forties in the process of resolving their developmental crisis. They cannot put it off until next week, next month, next year; they want the weight off now!

Many find the initial period of dieting exceedingly difficult. It is not the first day or two that is hard to get through, but the third, the fourth, the fifth. There often comes a bitter moment on the scale when they discover a week's suffering has resulted in the loss of a mere pound or two—whereas they had anticipated something more like a five- or even ten-pound loss. In their thirties this frustration might well have triggered a whole series of explanations that would have safely short-circuited further dieting, rationalizations such as "There's just something wrong with my metabolism"; "I'm one of those who simply can't lose weight"; "I'm not meant to be thin." But in her early forties, she is much less likely to be fooled by her own mind games, and back she goes to the grinding task of curbing her caloric intake.

After a while she begins to see results, and in addition to the satisfaction of actually losing weight, she experiences the exhilaration of achieving a difficult goal through self-control.

A forty-three-year-old woman, who had a long history of diets tried and failed, described her recently successful efforts to lose weight.

The turning point for me was a bedroom mirror we put up. I told my husband we ought to return it. It was as bad as one of those fun-house mirrors they have in amusement parks. I was sure it was distorting. Then my son said it was a great mirror, and he would take it if I didn't want it. It wasn't the mirror; it was my figure.

That did it. I like food; I love to cook; I love to give dinner parties. I love new recipes. Those days are over. No one thought me, of all people, could change a lifetime of eating habits. I wondered myself how strong I could be. I surprised even myself. It was murder those first weeks. Not a pound came off. I didn't give up. I have counted every shred of lettuce I eat. I memorized calorie books. It's taken time. I never thought it would take so long. That isn't how it is. Five months now. I know that when I'm down to where I want to be, I can't go back to my old eating habits. I can't tell you how good I feel. It's obvious now. I wouldn't have dreamed of putting on a pants suit last year, and you should see the one I just bought.

One funny thing happened. One morning I was feeling especially thin. I could almost dig my fingers around my rib cage. I went into the bathroom eager to get on that scale before breakfast. I looked down and let out one scream. The whole family came running. My son had pulled a trick on me and had adjusted the scale to weigh fifteen pounds heavier. I had been half asleep and hadn't checked—just stepped on the scale, leaning a bit backward because on our scale you weigh lighter that way, and then I looked down. He caught on fast enough that his mother doesn't appreciate jokes about weight.

As she focuses greater attention on her body, a woman in her early forties probably realizes that losing weight is not the only means of achieving reconditioning. Over the years, some muscles probably have been used very little, have sagged, become flabby, and she may feel a general loss of muscle tone, a lack of graceful vigor. At thirty or thirty-five she wasn't trying out for any Olympic team, and whatever strength and agility she had were probably enough to meet the physical demands of her everyday life. In her forties, it is not a matter of merely being strong and agile enough to get through her daily activities. Feeling flabby, tired, graceless means feeling old. To regain her sense of vigor, she might begin a program of exercise—join a health club, enroll in a gym class, begin practicing yoga, become involved in some sport such as swimming, tennis, or golf.

If she has not recently been engaged in vigorous physical activity, the initial reaction to her new program of exercise is anything but encouraging. With sore muscles she probably feels even clumsier than before, and rather than immediately regaining a firm and graceful body, she might spend the first few weeks aching and limping. After a while, the aches recede, the limping stops, she gains a feeling of energetic liveliness that she hasn't experienced in years.

A forty-two-year-old woman, the mother of three children, as well as a part-time real estate salesperson, described her experience with tennis.

I had to do something. I thought of gym classes, but the idea of spending an hour searching for my toes didn't send me into ecstasy. A few of us got together and had the great idea of taking up tennis. It's kind of the "in" thing to do. It was hard starting over. I had played years ago, but after not having been near a court in over ten years I felt like a horse with lead feet.

The worst was the group on the adjoining court. I would have given anything for a brick wall between us.

There were these young girls swishing around hitting the ball back and forth, and on the next court four "ladies." Luckily we were determined to continue playing. It's been a lot better each time. I find the movements come back. Lately it's been a lot of fun. My body hasn't felt as good in years.

People of all ages occasionally buy new clothes as a means of combating moodiness or depression. There is no need to overinterpret this normal phenomenon. Thus, when reaching forty and feeling depressed about her age, a woman may turn to buying as one way of raising her spirits.

A woman who had recently turned forty described her own behavior at this stage—and her reaction to the comment of a young salesperson.

I felt like hell. It just hit me—waves of depression, all because I was turning forty. I felt like I was being driven up a wall. I know rationally how silly it is. Somehow being thirty-nine wasn't so bad; the idea of being forty threw me completely. My husband insisted we celebrate. He said I would feel better if we went out and had a binge. No thanks. I wanted no part of that kind of celebration.

I remember when I was in my twenties—the girls all talked about being forty as if it meant one foot in the grave. I think it's terrible the way we get conditioned to seeing an age in that way. I had to do something. It was insanity, I suppose, besides being expensive, but I took practically every stitch of clothing I owned and gave it to a thrift shop. I went out and bought a complete wardrobe. Everything—you name it. It was a fabulous experience except for one thing. I was trying on a dress, and the salesgirl came into the room. She said to me, "I've never seen that dress on an *older* woman. It looks good. It's a popular number with college girls." I felt like crawling out of the store. I guess it shows. What I hate more than anything is how friends and people I meet seem to bring up age more now than I ever remember. It seems as if everyone wants to make sure you face how old you're getting.

Enhancing one's appearance entails a good deal more than the impulse buying initially displayed when a woman reaches forty. Later on, as she begins to respond more constructively to the pressures of this stage, rather than using shopping sprees as a defense mechanism for dealing with moments of moodiness, she may begin to further develop her sense of style, expand her knowledge of fabrics and design, and learn to select clothes that are most appropriate for her particular figure and personality. With practice, she may acquire the skill to use fashion as an effective technique for coping with aging.

A forty-four-year-old woman who has a teen-aged daughter contrasted her own efforts in buying clothes with the ease of her daughter's shopping.

My daughter will walk into a store, take anything from the inexpensive racks, put it on and walk out looking like a million dollars. I wasn't any different at her age. Now when I shop it's an expedition. I have to hunt. This dress doesn't camouflage the places on me that need camouflaging. I can't have too much behind showing, and certainly I have to watch the front. I don't put on a six-inch-wide belt and go prancing out. The dress has to fall wide where I am wide.

I was shopping with a friend last week, and everything we tried on we had one reaction—the outfit didn't do anything for us. That's the way with clothes now. They have to build you up, do something for you. Looking good isn't that easy. When you're over forty you need good fabrics, good cuts—otherwise you look sleazy. Getting old is an expensive proposition. I like to look nice. I really do. I find, though, it takes a lot more time and energy to find the right styles. It's no longer a matter of throwing anything on and hoping for the best.

The First Gray Hair

"One by one I pulled them out."

If weight is the most common of the physical concerns of the woman in her early forties, surely gray hair ranks a close second. A forty-one-year-old woman who works for a public relations firm talked about how the onset of gray hair made her feel she was entering a new stage of life.

It's odd how something can happen to you as a child, and you forget about it until years later. I had an aunt who some of the family used to make fun of behind her back. Fat, forty, and an old maid, or some such remarks. Even as a child, I recognized how mean they were.

I used to spend a lot of time with her. I remember one evening in particular—I was about nine or ten— she was in her bedroom, and she called to me. I went in. She was standing looking into a mirror, and she had a tweezers in one hand. It looked to me like she was about to stab herself. I was honestly scared for a moment until she asked if I would help her pull gray hairs.

It was hard for her to see the back of her head. I stood there plucking out gray hairs one by one.

She told me that she had heard from a friend's mother that if you pulled out gray hairs as soon as they came in you stopped them from spreading or even growing. She had beautiful dark red hair. I remember her sitting in a chair, bent over, and this mass of hair falling over her face. I parted and hunted for gray hairs. "It will happen to you at forty, just you wait," she warned me.

I forgot all about that time until recently when I was looking into a bathroom mirror and I happened to notice a few gray hairs. I automatically reached for a tweezers. One by one I pulled them out. Almost thirty years later I was doing exactly the same thing as my aunt. It made me feel very strange. I realized that it was just a beginning—the start of the whole bit, rinses, touch-ups, trips to the beauty shop. Maybe I'm the kind who overdramatizes things, but it seemed to me at that moment, gray hairs initiated me into the forties. I was getting old.

In our youth-oriented society, many women associate gray hair with a loss of attractiveness. In describing her husband's reactions to her gray hair, a forty-one-year-old woman expressed her own feelings.

I know he hates my gray hair. He never comes right out and says anything directly. From comments he's made about other women, I know he must feel that way about me. I don't like it either, though I hate the idea of becoming a slave to beauty shops. My hair is getting impossible since it turned gray. When the color goes, hair seems to change texture. It's stiff now, doesn't take a curl. I could have it up all night in rollers, and the next morning it just hangs limp. I dread summers because of the way it hangs in strings.

I don't think I envy young girls, except for one thing —their hair. That's how my hair was when I was a teen-ager. It hung nearly to my waist, and sun gave it blond streaks. All I did was run a comb through after swimming. I could do anything with it. Now I can pull, twist, roll, pin it, and nothing helps. It's like trying to do something with cardboard.

Obviously, gray hair itself is neither intrinsically beautiful nor ugly. The judgment depends upon one's point of view. If a thirty-year-old woman discovers a few strands of gray, she probably feels it is *pre*mature, and without much fuss or bother removes the strands, uses a rinse, or just forgets about it. But from the perspective of the early forties, the same few strands of hair may have enormous psychological import. They reenforce her culturally determined belief that, having passed the age of forty, she is well on the way to drab middle age.

Sexual Rejection

"I'm not a Bunny girl. I am his wife."

A married woman in her early forties is confronted not only by her own concerns about aging, but also by her husband's problems. If he is somewhere in his early to middle forties, his emotional reactions are probably fairly severe and disturbing. And his behavior is likely to reenforce her own growing concerns about herself.

As we have seen, her husband, at this stage in his development, is becoming increasingly aware of his mortality, his physical limitations and disabilities. He is probably anxious about losing his sexual potency, worried about his career, and examining the choices made earlier in his life. With a mounting sense of pressure, he looks back at the person he has been, he looks forward to the person he wants to be, and he comes to feel that this is his last chance to fulfill lifelong dreams, ideals, and goals.

Under any conditions, it would not be easy to live with a man who is facing the onset of an identity crisis. He may withdraw from the family, become anxious, depressed, irritable, and egocentric. But when a wife is in her early forties, precisely because of her own developmental crisis, she is especially vulnerable to her husband's behavior. Given her own concerns at this stage of life, she cannot help feeling that his behavior represents a rejection of her. She may be hurt and angry at him, but she is still likely to feel that any disruption of their sexual relations is a consequence of her own loss of seductive appeal. She tries even harder, becomes more attentive, more seductive, but he often fails to respond, and her frustration grows worse.

She may recognize the stresses he is under, his self-doubts. But sometimes, no matter how hard she tries, she cannot seem to reach him. She may strive to be sympathetic and understanding; she may even consciously appreciate the fact that his problems stem from sources outside of their relationship. But more often than not, despite this conscious realization, at a deeper and more irrational level, she believes that his difficulties somehow reflect the consequences of her own aging.

The wish to be young again is reflected in the remarks of a forty-three-year-old woman who talked about her problems with her husband.

The way things were going, I finally had to ask him. It isn't easy to come out and ask the person you're married to why he doesn't find you much of a bed partner any more. He didn't want to talk about it much. He told me to take a good look at myself and I'd find out the answer without him going into details. I guess at the end of a day of putting away laundry, going to the grocery store, straightening up the house, chauffeuring kids, I'm not a temptress—a sex siren. Frankly, at my age, I'd feel like a damn fool getting into a sheer nightgown, climbing into bed and acting like one. Maybe when I was younger it was different—then, too, you're not self-conscious, and you can act a bit. Now I feel I've been through a mill—kids' problems, his worries, my own problems—and I feel foolish. Of course, I enjoy sex. I enjoyed it because I thought it was a way the two of us came closer together. We never needed the build up. Sex was part of our lives, naturally, and it didn't depend on nightgowns or the right atmosphere.

I have this feeling he's had too much TV—too much of the sex magazines the boys have up in their rooms. I know that sounds silly, but that's how I see it. I'm not a Bunny girl. I am his wife, the mother of his children, the cook and bottle washer. And I'm forty years old. It depresses me terribly. You feel like a child with a wish. You wish you could turn back time and be young again. Life is very real, and to slip into fantasy at bedtime seems fake to me.

I'd like to be wanted; I'd like him to give a little and take me for what I am now, the way I look. I know that I accept him—thinning hair, extra pounds, naps in the afternoon in front of the TV. He's not a teen-ager anymore. I'd think he could accept me as I am. It doesn't seem I'm asking too much.

She may feel that if she could only regain her youthful figure, her husband would be attracted to her. If she could only regain the color and texture of her youthful hair, she would be appealing to him. If she could only regain her youthful energy and vivacity, she would reawaken his interest.

Consciously, of course, she recognizes that these are absurd, irrational wishes. Although they may occasionally occur to her in dreams and fantasies, they are generally repressed in her waking life, and in her interactions with her husband she is more likely to express overtly her frustration and anger. Notwithstanding the legitimacy of these feelings, in a strange twist of emotions, she may also feel an underlying sense of guilt about the fact that she is aging.

Her culturally derived perspective leads her to interpret her experiences in a way that reenforces her fear of aging, so that when her husband withdraws from her sexually as a result of his own developmental problems, she is prone to interpret this as a rejection of her because she is growing older.

Because the early-forties woman often sees the difficulties of her sexual life with her husband as her own fault—a consequence of her own loss of attractiveness—she may be unusually sensitive to the ways in which other men relate to her.

Typical is the comment of a forty-three-year-old business woman about an apparent increase in "respectful behavior" among her male colleagues.

You have to face it. After forty the men at the office you've worked with for years treat you differently. It's not so subtle. We hold a lot more business meetings at the office instead of going out to lunch. There's more going off in separate directions. I can remember a few years ago we might drop into a bar after work and sit around and talk—even the married fellows joined us. Now they still go out, but I got the message that I wasn't welcome. They couldn't have been louder or clearer. Women my age don't do that sort of thing. It's O.K. for the thirties, but not an older woman. She is supposed to go right home after work and hop into bed by ten-thirty.

It keeps popping up—the feeling of being cut off. The young men, and they're not that much younger than I am, sort of pull themselves up and become respectful when I'm there. It's not a matter of ten, fifteen years difference I'm talking about. It's me over forty and them under forty. Lines are drawn and I didn't draw them.

Work and the Problem of Promotion

"I've proven myself. That means I work twice as hard as any man."

If the woman in her early forties has been working, by this time she has probably reached a point in her career at which she feels that a significant advancement is due. Some of her male colleagues have probably already been promoted, and she begins to feel that it is time for her to receive some recognition. She has more than likely experienced some discrimination on the job because of her sex, but she has worked hard, accomplished a good deal, and perhaps feels that in her particular work setting she can reasonably expect a reward for her efforts. At this stage in her career, however, she may well experience even greater frustration than she has before.

A business executive in her forties talked about the difficulties she had encountered.

It was twenty years before I got a break and moved into management. I can't count the times young men without my background and experience walked into positions with twice my salary and prestige. I thought about leaving. Somehow the years passed. I was in a rut. Then, too, I had built up seniority and a pension. It isn't easy to throw away all these things. I have to help support my parents. I'm not married, so at least there aren't children to worry about.

What makes me furious, even more than the men, are women who sleep their way up the ladder. It's a fact. That's one sure way for a fast promotion. I'm not doing this. You have to remember I'm from a different era. Maybe if I were starting out in today's world I wouldn't be so hung up on the morality I was raised with. I don't know. I do know for a fact that women today coming right from college have it a lot easier than I ever had. They know their way around a lot more.

Despite the problems she has had to deal with, as a function of her own abilities plus the slowly changing attitudes toward working women, by the time she reaches her early forties, she may achieve some degree of status and recognition. At this stage, however, she is likely to discover that, as she moves up the scale of career advancement, further progress becomes increasingly difficult. She finds that each step upward is steeper than the preceding one. It is almost as if there were an implicit rule that says women can advance just so far—and then no further.

There is no single definition of this point for various kinds of work, but when the next advance means that the early-forties woman will be in a position to exercise significant power over men in her age group, she is likely to discover that this step is the steepest of all in her career. Women have their place as secretaries, clerks, sales people, even assistant managers, lower-level executives. But despite whatever changes have occurred as a result of the movement for women's liberation, by and large the world of upper-echelon executives is still reserved for men. If a business woman's ambitions are aimed at entering this realm of status and power, she may well feel cheated and disappointed.

One woman who did achieve a great deal of success in the world of business discussed some of the problems she had met.

I've had to fight behind the scenes and on the scene for every promotion and every raise I've gotten. I know it's because I'm a woman. I was working before women's liberation became a fad. I know what they're talking about. I lived through it before it was fashionable. A friend of mine told me to use feminine tactics to beat the game. I resent that. I have my integrity. I know I have talent. I've proven myself. That means I also work twice as hard as any man. I always have.

It's nothing you can put your finger on exactly, in the day-to-day work. It has shown up when managerial positions open up, and I'm passed over. The only time there was a shift was when our firm was threatened. We were going to lose some big government contracts unless there was a woman in a top position. I have never seen such quick action. Within forty-eight hours I was called in, promoted, and moved to a big office. You know, the victory came too late for it to really mean much to me. Of course, I am pleased. I'm human, though the success is still tainted by those past years when I sweated my way, and nothing happened. I'm not resentful. Progress has been made. There's still a long way to go before women can truly be on equal footing.

The Single Woman

"I guess if I were perfectly honest I'd say looking ahead sometimes does make me uncomfortable."

The single woman obviously doesn't have to deal with a husband facing the onset of his own identity crisis. In this respect, she is under considerably less strain than many married women in their forties. Nevertheless, she does encounter other stresses, many of which derive from the way others see her and relate to her. For a variety of reasons, she tends to be "set aside" by her married friends, and the fact that she is not married seems to be emphasized by them even more than before. This may be a consequence of the tension her friends are beginning to experience in their own marriages at this time. Her married female friends may see her as a possible rival for their husbands' affections. This fear is usually unfounded, not only because few women are sexually stimulated by their friends' husbands but also because troubled husbands are probably not the most cheerful company for a forty-year-old single woman and usually "handle" their troubles by focusing their libidinal attention on younger women.

Whatever the reasons might be, the single woman in her early forties often finds that her married friends are no longer as cordial as they once were. In most instances, this doesn't represent a large part of her circle of friends; married people tend to be friendly with other married people and single people tend to be friendly with other single people. Nevertheless, the shifts in her married friends' ways of relating to her have some effect on her social life, as an experience described by an attorney, a single woman in her early forties, shows.

To the rest of the world I'm an unmarried fortyish old maid. It burns me. No one ever talks about just being a single gal. It's always in relationship to a man. Men are bachelors. No one talks about a man in his forties as being unmarried in the same way they talk about women. I know I'm being defensive. I wasn't open to marriage. I ran around a lot. I had my chances to get married; I wasn't interested. I'm still not sure.

I hear some of the married women I know talking about their problems—their kids, drugs, dropouts, husbands cheating on them—and I've even had a couple of women say to me they are sure I don't know how lucky I am. I've worked hard to get my position. I like my freedom. I decide where I'm going and what I'm going to do with my money. I'm sure my wanting it this way has something to do with the way my mother was. She was scared of her own shadow when it came to my father. He really treated her with an iron hand. If that was marriage, I wanted no part of it.

I like men and I like women, too. For years I had a very active social life, but something changed when I turned forty. I had this feeling I was dropped from the social list. I never am invited as the odd girl any more to a party or dinner. Men my age who aren't married still rate on party lists. That bothers me. I wonder if the people were really my friends. I find now my social circle narrowing off. I'm put in the same basket as the divorcées. Married couples want you to keep further away than a ten-foot pole.

I don't want to have a roommate, another woman. I like my independence. I do get lonely. I think the real jolt came when my parents died. They didn't live near me, but at holidays I always went to visit. Their home was a base. They died last year, and this last Christmas was very rough. My nieces and nephews are young kids. I invited them to visit, though I didn't think they'd come. They live on the other side of the country. I thought about going out there and changed my mind. It was a very difficult Christmas. The fact that I survived helped me to see I could make it alone.

I need to do some thinking now, I suppose. I've made up my mind I have to push myself. I've considered joining some clubs. I suppose there are lots like me —men too, I'm sure. Suddenly you reach a point and you say to yourself, "O.K., you're forty-two; you've achieved; now what?"

The theme of aloneness occurs again and again in the comments of single women at this stage of life. While being alone is by no means the same as loneliness, they are frequently concerned about the possibility of becoming lonely as they grow older. In fact, the threat of future loneliness is the most common source of stress mentioned by single women in their early forties.

Women freely and openly discuss this problem far more often than men, though most likely it is no less of a problem for men. The difference is probably due to the fact that, in our culture, it is more acceptable for a woman to show feelings of loneliness.

These feelings are expressed in the comments of a forty-three-year-old woman who was in charge of office personnel for a major insurance company.

I'm always amused when people ask me if I'm lonely. I guess they assume that if you live alone you're lonely. That's far from the truth. The only peace and quiet I get with the kind of life I lead is when I get into the apartment and lock the door and pull the telephone jack. A few hours to myself are a precious commodity. I enjoy it all. I wouldn't do it if I really didn't find it satisfying. That doesn't mean I don't treasure a few hours to myself.

I wouldn't dream of changing my present life-style. I guess if I were perfectly honest with myself, I'd say looking ahead sometimes does make me uncomfortable. That's only happened recently, though. I know exactly what started me thinking. People at the office collected food and gifts for a nursing home in our area. I was on the committee and went over to bring the stuff. That afternoon bothered me. It had nothing to do with conditions. It was a lovely place. The people were alert and sweet. It shouldn't have depressed me. I told myself if conditions were bad, the people in poor health, I could have understood feeling upset. That wasn't the case.

I sat with this dear little lady for a bit, and we talked. She told me she had been a singer and a dancer and I saw her scrapbook of clippings—some little theater companies, nothing big. She wasn't at all unhappy—just wanted to talk. She didn't have any close family. She showed me a post card she had gotten from a grandniece who was in Paris and a handkerchief from some other person who had known her cousin.

It wasn't the woman—it was me. I got this awful feeling of seeing myself alone as she was. I tried not to show it, but I couldn't get away fast enough. I made all sorts of promises to myself that I would be her foster relative. I sent her a bed jacket. I've never gone back.

It wasn't that I can't face her; I can't face myself in that situation—alone.

The view that all, or even most, single women in their early forties want to be married is not supported by our observations. For many of them, remaining single was the result of a conscious, rational decision. They were interested in pursuing a career and felt that it couldn't be combined with marriage and a family; they had simply not been "ready for marriage"; or they had just never met anyone they wanted to marry. However, at this point, they often begin to reconsider their position. Perhaps they feel that, given the American culture's view of aging, they are reaching a time that represents a "last chance" to decide whether they wish to be married. They may rethink this question for some time and then decide that they really do prefer their single status. Some, however, revise their previous views and consider the possibility of marriage. One factor in the shift may be that their lives as single people have actually changed. By and large, early-forties women are no longer involved in the life of the "swinging singles." They usually feel, for example, that the singles' bars are for younger people, and they may be uncomfortable about joining social groups designed to introduce "singles." If they do participate in groups, it is usually ones organized around some particular recreational or intellectual activity, such as theater or music.

A successful advertising executive in her early forties described her evolving feelings about marriage.

I turned down plenty of chances to get married; I liked my independence. I didn't want to be tied down washing someone else's clothes, cooking meals. I liked my career, and frankly I never had problems about promotion. I know there are a lot of horror stories about

women being discriminated against. Somehow I wasn't
affected. I have training and talent. I am good, damn
good, and I was recognized.

I liked lots of the men I dated—never enough to
want to give up my job, and that's what marriage
means. I don't think you can be a part-time wife,
mother, and professional. Something has to give.
I'm not sorry about my decision. I wasn't open to
marriage and I knew it. I think people are ready to
get married at different ages. With me it has been
late. I think I am ready, and there aren't many
available men my age.

I know what happened in my case. I had my parents,
and I think they filled more of my life than I realized.
I lost them both within a year; for the first time I felt
alone. Even if I didn't see them I knew they were there,
and I could call. Their deaths were a turning point for
me. I was alone. A few cousins scattered around the
country—that's about it. I've lost touch with them. I
have a sister. She's having enough troubles in her second marriage, and I never was close to her children.
They're off in college. I send gifts, but that's all there
is to the relationship.

Suddenly, I realize I'm thrown more and more with
the singles, and men are out of that circle. It's not my
style. Dinner and theater with the girls leaves me cold.
I'd honestly like to meet someone. I think now if I met
the right guy, I'd throw the whole career over. I've had
my successes and am ready for something else.

Reactivating the Mind: School, Work, Community

"All I know is I'm out of the house, and I'm beginning to feel like a new person."

If she has devoted the previous ten or fifteen years to raising a family, the woman in her early forties may now well have a sense of intellectual stultification. Her children are probably making fewer demands on her time and energy. She has much more freedom to pursue her own educational interests. Some women return to school at this point, with a high level of success both in terms of actual academic achievement as well as subjective feelings of accomplishment and intellectual growth.

A forty-three-year-old woman who had left college when she was married described her feelings about going back to school.

I reached a point where I had to get out of the house. I felt meaningless. It got to a point where I envied my children. They had things to do. My husband has his work. I was left taking care of the house. I told them all they would have to help out. I wasn't going to fade away into a blob on the wall. The best thing I ever did for myself was to enroll in a course in an extension program. I did better than I thought I would. It changed my whole life. The idea of having someplace to go to once a week, away from the family, grocery stores, laundry, made a huge difference in my life. I decided to keep going. They're going to be surprised when someday I'll finish all the credits for a degree. At this point I'm not even thinking about what I'll do with the degree. I just am glad to do something with my mind instead of staying home and vegetating.

With increased freedom from the daily demands of child-rearing, some women find the most significant response to the stress of this period is a return to work. They are not necessarily concerned, at least initially, with pursuing a career, though their success on the job may well lead in this direction. Most important, in addition to the economic rewards, is the opportunity to discover the value of being engaged in productive work outside the home.

A forty-four-year-old woman who hadn't held a job in nearly twenty years talked about her excitement at returning to work.

I knew I had to get out and do something with myself. The kids don't need me at home. They're in school and busy after school with their own activities. The days were dragging. I felt that I'd go out of my mind with one more luncheon, card party, or club meeting. I've lost my enthusiasm for those things. I want to do something more meaningful.

My training is horrible. When I was in college the idea was to get a general education. Four years of sociology and literature and subjects like that, and you've improved yourself, but you haven't anything marketable. I don't even have a teaching license. I wish I had had more direction. I was just groping, and then I fell into something and I'm terribly excited. It's a beginning. One of the people in town has a small business, and he needed someone to manage the office a few hours a day. I meet people, do some typing, answer phones. I couldn't care what I did. All I know is I'm out of the house and I'm beginning to feel like a new

person. It's the change. Eventually I plan on going back
to school and getting some training. Right now this has
been perfect to start me off.

For some women, neither returning to school nor to a job
is appealing. Instead, they may find involvement in community activities rewarding. Local school and government
affairs, social, charitable, and religious organizations—a
good deal of the energy and talent necessary for these activities comes from women in their early forties who are responding to their developmental crisis by finding worthwhile pursuits.

A woman of forty-three, a member of her local board of
education and a very active participant in a variety of school
activities, talked about her current project with enormous
enthusiasm.

It's been a very busy year for me. Either I get away for
a few days soon or I'll drop in my tracks. Someone has
to take on responsibilities. The women are willing to
help, but they're always ready with excuses. We've just
had a run of activities. The Spring Carnival for the
school is our biggest affair. I've been up nights calling
people, getting donations. People have no idea what is
involved to get these things under way. I haven't gotten
more than six hours' sleep in the past month. We
depend on the proceeds for the library and the art
department.

I've been sick about what happened, though. One of
our biggest donors just called and told me he can't give
us a donation this year for the door prize. For the last
five years he has given us a portable television set. This
year he said he had to cut back on all his gifts. His
children are at the school. I can't believe he's telling
the truth. They're always flying off for vacations. There
isn't anything we can do, and the brochures were

printed. We'll have to get something as a substitute.
It's hard work but I love it. Each year I say I won't do
it again, and then I'm asked and I accept. There is a
good feeling, though, when it's all over and the evening
is a success.

The Affair

"My husband travels a lot."

We have no systematic basis for estimating the frequency
of extramarital affairs among women in their early forties,
and we do not mean to imply that it is a common phenomenon. However, these affairs seem to occur somewhat more
frequently at this stage than earlier. They can be seen as one
response to the psychological crisis being faced.

To a certain extent, these extramarital experiences are
motivated by a wife's need for reaffirmation of her own sense
of self-worth and attractiveness. They are often associated
with a history of a husband's earlier rejection; he may be
egocentrically concerned with his own problems, over-
whelmingly involved in his work, sullenly withdrawn and
depressed. In any event, his wife is likely to interpret his
behavior as a rejection of herself because she is aging and less
attractive. Thus, she may be particularly susceptible to the
attentions of another man who reaffirms her sense of her
own desirability.

Although extramarital activities represent a departure
from traditional standards of marriage, the comments of

women who discussed these experiences generally revealed not only a naïve romanticism, but a rather conventional set of values about such relationships. For example, they apparently apply the same kind of demand for monogamous fidelity that is conventionally associated with marriage. We do not believe that this reflects any innate biological preference in either men or women for monogamous sexual relationships. It undoubtedly reflects acquired cultural values. Nevertheless, it does indicate the degree to which conventional values and expectations influence ostensibly unconventional behaviors.

In discussing a recent experience she had while in a local drama group, a woman in her early forties described a relationship she had had with one of the men in the group.

I have been very active in lots of community affairs. I've got to fill evenings. My husband travels a lot. He's been out of town a couple of weeks every month. I got into this theater group at our community center and auditioned for a play. I had done some theater in college, nothing very serious. I have no illusions about my theater work. I've always been considered a ham when I'm wound up. I never expected to get the lead.

It was a fantastic experience. We must have rehearsed at least four months. All of the cast became very close. That's typical of theater people, though. It's hard not to relate in this way when you're constantly together for rehearsals.

The leading man and I had a lot of big scenes, and he couldn't always get to night rehearsals because his business stayed open three nights a week. He and I tried to get a few hours in during the day. It was easier for him to come to my house. The gossip mongers in our area infuriated me. We did need the time together —the scenes demanded perfect timing, and my feeling is if you go into a production you do it seriously, amateur or not. We worked beautifully together.

The show was a success—sellout for both nights, and we had to give an extra performance. After all those months, breaking up was horrible. I really miss rehearsals. He and I were perfect for our roles. We thought we'd do another play. I called him and suggested we try out a run-through of a musicale which might go over in our community. He didn't show up. I don't know whether I should call and find out what happened. I'm hurt in a way. We had become very close, and it's been very empty since the show closed.

The Pressure to Change

"I wasn't going to fade away into a blob on the wall."

In the course of growing up, every woman has learned from others in her culture that forty is a crucial watershed, an age that separates young adulthood from maturity. It is more than a change from one chronological age to another, for this particular stage of development carries with it an enormous overload of emotional meaning. It may mean an end of youthful vigor, and she may feel that she is but a quick, short step from dull and dreary middle age.

Having learned to view the forties this way, she is predisposed to interpret her experiences within the context of her own aging. Thus, she is likely to feel that an added inch or two around her waist is a sure sign of her slide toward dreary middle age—just as the first gray hairs, the suggestion of crow's-feet, the hint of a double chin, the normal aches and pains of everyday living are seen as signs of the loss of youthful attractiveness.

If she is married, she faces the problems engendered by a husband living through his own developmental crisis. And to some extent, regardless of her rational understanding of his problems, she may interpret his behavior as a rejection of her because she is aging. In addition, she believes that younger people are beginning to see her and treat her differently—as one of the "older generation." If she has been pursuing a career, she may feel at this point the added frustration of failing to achieve the kind of advancement she believes she has earned. And if she is single she may ponder a future of growing old alone.

For many years, she has seen herself with little or no change in her age role. She has thought of herself as a "young adult," with all of the physical and social characteristics usually associated with that term. Now, within a relatively brief period of time, she feels compelled to change this aspect of her self-concept.

It is quite easy for her to feel threatened by the pressure to change her view of herself. After all, in some respects the change implies giving up a self-image that she has had for many years. But then, after an initial period of more or less anxious concern, she usually resolves this dilemma before it gains the momentum of a major crisis. Despite the potentially severe ego threat involved, the great majority of women come through the crisis by the end of their early forties without undue strain.

The efforts to resolve this developmental crisis may take a variety of directions. A woman might focus on dieting and physical reconditioning; she might pay greater attention to her clothes and make-up; she might become more active in community affairs, get a job, take some courses. The stresses encountered at this stage often lead to a period of significant psychological growth because she tends to take an active stance in responding to them. By virtue of responding actively, she may develop new interests and skills, an enhanced sense of self-worth, and a greater zest for living.

In reacting to the crisis of the early forties, a woman both accepts and modifies the cultural view of aging. On the one hand, despite her initial apprehensiveness, she tends to adopt the view that she has reached a certain stage of maturity and is no longer a young adult. On the other hand, she usually discovers that the stereotypical characteristics associated with the forties in our culture need not apply to her. In fact, given her active response to this crisis, by the end of the early forties she is likely to be slimmer, dressed more attractively, in better physical condition, more energetic and intellectually active than she was when she turned forty. Thus, this stage of development usually represents a time of increasing psychological strength—strength that she will need as she meets the crisis ahead.

middle forties

The Supportive Wife

"I'm jumping through hoops trying to make sense of what he expects."

Following the crisis of the early forties, there is often a period of relatively high satisfaction, involving a good deal of activity outside the home and family. The length of this period obviously varies, depending upon factors such as the individual's psychological integration, the problems faced by her husband and children, and the amount of stress from other sources. Sometimes this plateau of busy satisfaction lasts only a few months; for others it may continue for two or three years. Sooner or later, however, problems are encountered that generate a crisis that is typically more severe than that of the early forties. Moving into the middle forties is often the beginning of this crisis.

Although she may be involved in many different activities, a woman's fundamental sense of self derives from a complex set of interrelationships with significant others—husband, children, parents.

When she is in her mid-forties, these relationships most likely undergo a transformation. In view of the fact that she has defined herself largely in terms of these roles—wife, mother, daughter—any changes that occur can be threatening. She begins to experience self-doubt and apprehension about her psychological integration. The marital difficulties encountered at this stage may impose a severe strain on her identity.

During the middle forties a husband is likely to be living through an extraordinarily stressful period in his own psychological development, and his wife often suffers the slings and arrows of his sometimes outrageous behavior. A wife's initial response to her husband's problems is usually one of sympathetic concern and reassurance. But she may find it difficult at first to fully grasp the depth of his disturbance. On the surface, at least, his life doesn't seem to have changed radically enough to warrant the dramatic change in his behavior. She knows that he has been worried about his business, concerned about his health, bothered by an apparent decrease in sexual drive. Nevertheless, having recently gone through her own developmental crisis of the early forties and overcome it by taking an active, energetic stance, she may assume that her husband is facing the same kind of problems and will soon grow out of them.

However, he doesn't grow out of his problems—not just yet. In fact, things usually get much worse before they get better; meanwhile, she suffers through a variety of his emotional reactions. The most blatant are his explosions of anger. Often provoked by apparently trivial issues, the outbursts seem to feed on themselves, anger leading to increasing anger. During these moments of rage he may accuse his wife of just about anything, often dredging up the past to recite a catalogue of her mistakes.

This experience was described by a forty-four-year-old woman who was currently suffering through her husband's explosions of hostility.

I can't have changed that much. He screams at me that I'm a completely different person from the woman he married. The way he behaves at times, I think he's done the changing. I never explode like that. There seems to be no reason for his outbursts. I can look the wrong way, and that will send him off in a rage. He will pick on some small thing I've done or said which was just in passing, and he'll build it up into a monumental issue. If I ask him a simple thing like fix a window catch, and he doesn't, and I remind him, then I'm a nag.

I don't know what he wants any more. I feel like I'm jumping through hoops trying to make sense of what he expects. What hurts me more than anything else is when he blames me for every problem, every crisis, every failure he has. I spent years helping him. When he was going through graduate school I held a job—and, God, I hated the work I did—but I did it for a long-range goal. When he went into a business I went down during the day and helped out. Who did the books for him? Who still answers telephones?

I'm not trying to picture myself as a martyr, but to blame me for every problem is unfair. It isn't my fault that a deal he's been working on fell through. I had nothing to do with it. He turned on me and said it was my fault. If he had a decent home life, a wife who meant something to him, a wife who helped, he could have gone out and clinched the deal. Everything ends up being my fault. I get terribly tired of this role. I can't cope any more.

One morning I didn't have my hair just so. I had a terrible headache. I couldn't sleep, and I guess I looked dragged out. He didn't miss that shot. I got it. According to him, I am always a mess. He's embarrassed by me. The names he called me—slob, witch. Deep down I still believe he's a basically fine person. I can't take his accusations. I wish I knew what to do. What's happening to us—to our marriage? Where will it end? Worse, how will it end?

The middle-forties wife frequently doesn't know how to respond. If she tries to be quiet, conciliatory, her behavior seems to make matters worse. If she responds with counter-hostility, the interaction may escalate to a degree of rage that is frightening to both her and her husband. If she tries to be reasonable, rational, logical, he may sweep aside her arguments with an even greater explosion of anger. Nothing seems to work—and she may be left in tears, shaken, stunned, and confused.

Growing Apart

"I suppose the day will come when we'll have homes for castoff wives where husbands put them out to pasture."

If the outbursts of anger are dramatic and obviously hurtful, perhaps the periods of loneliness are even more painful. For one reason or another, she may find that she and her husband are spending less and less time together. He is busy with his work, he has to travel, he simply stays away from home.

The feelings of loneliness she experienced are described by a forty-three-year-old woman whose husband spent a great deal of time away from home.

I can't be sure he isn't playing around. How would I know? He has to go out of town a great deal. He works for a national company, and there are always conferences. I tell him I'm getting lonely. I hate weekends he's away. I drag myself around the apartment. I'm sick of taking the kids off to museums Saturdays—somewhere, anywhere to get out.

It was very bad last Friday. I've never done this—I called his office to find out where he was. You know, he hadn't even told me the name of the hotel. His secretary had to tell me. I called him and had him paged. He got on the telephone, and I told him how I felt. I told him I was very unhappy, and he seemed sorry. There wasn't anything he could do. He said to "stay loose" and he'd be home on Tuesday on an early plane.

I was with some friends in the building that Saturday afternoon, and usually I never talk about my private life. This time I must have had a drink. I started crying, and I thought I would get some comfort. I was floored. One of the women told me that it's the same with her husband. She said what she does is get a sitter for the kids while she goes off and gets herself laid. I wonder if she realized what she was saying! She's a very beautiful woman. Her feeling is her husband is having his. She might as well have some fun, too. I don't want that kind of life.

Even when she and her husband are together, he may be shut off from her, unreachable behind a wall of sullen depression. She may try to breach the gap, but he is likely to retreat even further. She may try to devise shared activities, projects she feels might bring them closer. But no matter how ingenious her plans might be, she usually encounters little success. She may in fact try too hard—become too clever, too obviously seductive—and the result may simply be an increase of tension and discomfort. In any event, regardless of her efforts, she may sense her husband drifting away.

In talking about her marriage, a woman in her middle forties described this sense of growing apart.

I can feel he is slipping away from me, and I know it's not all my fault. I wonder what's wrong. We've been married twenty-two years. Four children. I was the one who raised them. He had to travel a lot those first years when they were young. I stayed home. Because someone doesn't go to business doesn't mean she's an idiot. My daughters are different from me. They tell me they won't be trapped. I never thought of myself as trapped.

I try to talk to him. He says I'm making up stories. I asked him what he thought of me and he said I'm a sort of nothing—whatever that means. He compares me to some of the women in his office who are my age. He calls them "swingers." Maybe next to them I don't show up well. I don't starve myself until I'm a bone. I don't girdle myself until I can't breathe. I'm doing my best, though I have to face it—when you're my age you sag in places, and there's not much you can do.

He would like to put me out of his life. He says I'm to stop playing the martyr role. Maybe I was a fool to sacrifice myself—to think of the children and him before I thought of myself. I told him I was ready to shift the role—play another part. He said anytime I want out I'm welcome to go. He won't stop me. That hurts me a lot. I don't know if I am able to go at life alone. The security of my family and my home has meant a lot to me. It's not easy after all these years to make a clean break. The government subsidizes everything else. I suppose the day will come when we'll have homes for castoff wives whose husbands have put them out to pasture.

At this stage of marital life—perhaps at nearly any stage —a couple's sexual life together is probably a fair barometer by which to evaluate the overall quality of their relationship. It is by no means perfectly accurate. There are marriages in which a satisfying sexual life is not accompanied by a generally happy relationship; undoubtedly there are marriages in which the opposite is the case. Nevertheless, if one were to select one aspect of married life as a gauge, sex would seem to be as good a choice as any.

This is particularly relevant to our consideration of the woman in her middle forties, for at this stage her sexual relationship with her husband is likely to be irregular, disturbed, and frustrating—a state of affairs that both reflects the more general disruption in their marriage and aggravates the situation.

A forty-six-year-old woman talked about the sexual problems she had met in her own marriage.

I should have known what was happening. Hindsight is always easier than foresight. We stopped having sexual relations about a year ago. He told me he just couldn't get aroused. I suggested he check with a doctor. Supposedly he did, and there was nothing wrong.

My husband said it was probably just overwork, exhaustion, and we'd have to wait it out. I accepted what he told me. After all, what proof did I have that it was anything else? You learn to live around the problem. After all, what happens in the bedroom isn't exactly a subject you can discuss with friends. The best thing to do is to keep up a front. We went out as usual. With other people, we were the same couple. Only, I knew differently.

I think it was less of a problem at the time with me because of other things that were going on. It's an age when problems are dumped in your lap, and you barely have enough energy to keep your head above water. I had too much going on to feel the need for sex. I was drained by the children at the time, and by my parents, who had to come to live with us after they became ill. I was on the go from morning until night, and sex wasn't a high priority. Getting through each day was just about all I could handle.

Now that he is gone and isn't coming back, I want desperately to turn the time backward. I had always wanted just a few hours of freedom. Now that I have all the free time I want in the world it's very, very hard, and more than anything is the loneliness. The children are off to school . . . my husband gone . . . I have the house alone, and the days are tolerable. It's the nights that are driving me out of my mind.

During this period of marriage, jealousy may become a major issue. Given the way her husband is acting, it is not at all unreasonable for a mid-forties woman to feel rejected. His behavior implicitly, and maybe even explicitly, conveys the message "I don't want you," and no matter how much she understands his problems, that message is hard to accept with equanimity. At the same time, he may also be showing signs of attraction to other women—and it is difficult for his wife to control her feelings of jealousy.

These feelings are expressed in the comments of a woman who had been married for nearly twenty years.

I never was the jealous type. There are some women I know who think every woman is out after their husbands. Not me. It's not that I'm blind. I thought I knew my husband pretty well. You don't sleep in the same bed with someone for nearly twenty years without some idea about the person. I've got some girl friends who told me I better keep my eyes open. I laughed them off until something happened recently which made me think twice.

I was planning a cocktail party—a big bash—one of those "pay back for all the affairs we've been invited to" kinds of deals. Usually my husband never gets involved. I mean, if I'm planning a dinner, I pretty well decide who to invite. I know the office people. This time he surprises me and asks me about the list. I showed it to him, never dreaming he'd come up with some names. He mentioned a young couple I hardly remembered meeting. I told him we had never been invited to their house, and besides they were much younger. He told me they were interesting people.

Then he tells me he ran into the woman a few weeks before. Evidently she works near his office and they met accidentally. He was kind of vague. I gathered they had lunch together, which sounded kind of strange to me until he explained he was going to lunch, and she happened to be going to the same place—some little French restaurant near his office. I've never been there myself, though I know he likes it for lunch when he doesn't have to go with anyone from the office and just wants to relax in a quiet place.

The more I listened to him talking, the more I wondered. I must have said something, because he got very angry and said I was making a mountain out of a molehill. He happened to bump into her once and that was it, and I was trying to build up a story. He has a hell of a lot more on his mind than a twenty-five-year-old woman whose husband was just a nice guy on his way up. Now, what did I want from him? We didn't talk about it any more. A few weeks before the party he asked me if I had invited the couple.

I never have lied to my husband before. This was one time I stood there, and with a perfectly straight face I told him I had called her and invited them. They had theater tickets and couldn't come. I don't know if what I did was wrong or right. There's nothing I can do now. I can't tell my husband I lied. I wonder if they'll run into each other again and he'll find out the truth.

Not every married woman in her middle forties goes through the extremes of marital battles, sense of rejection, and jealousy we have discussed here. The discord between husband and wife may be more polite and subdued; the growing apart and failure of communication may be more subtle; the feelings of jealousy may be less obvious. And of course in addition to the problems, there are likely to be many satisfying aspects of middle-forties marriage. Nevertheless, aggression and counteraggression, rejection and loneliness, and the reduction of mutual understanding are not uncommon at this stage of married life.

Divorce

"I didn't only lose a husband, I lost a whole way of life."

At one time in our society, when married couples suffered through periods of crisis, happily or unhappily the vast majority of them remained together. Some of them did not stay together psychologically; though they remained married, husband and wife went their own ways. With changing social mores, in recent years, divorce has become a much more acceptable way of dealing with marital problems.

Given the stress of mid-forties marriage, plus the growing acceptance of divorce, it is not at all surprising that a significant number of couples at least consider the possibility, and that many couples in their middle forties do in fact get divorced.

It is practically impossible in most instances to identify either the husband's or the wife's behavior as the primary reason for a divorce. Regardless of who takes the legal initiative, both are almost always involved in the complex patterns of motivation underlying the decision. In the arguments that typically precede such a decision, each may blame the other for their troubles. But if one were to investigate the motives of a particular couple, chances are that the causes of divorce would be found in the *interaction* between husband and wife rather than in the behavior of either one or the other.

However, there are usually certain precipitating events that can be pointed to as the ostensible "cause" of a divorce. The husband may have met another woman whom he wishes to marry; the wife may suddenly discover that she finds her marriage stultifying.

A forty-five-year-old graduate student reported the following.

I tell my friends I have three diplomas, two from the university and one from the divorce court. Maybe I should frame all three and hang them side by side. They really go hand in hand.

I couldn't wait to get married. I quit college after two years. At the time I didn't have one regret. The only reason I went to college was to get a husband. The next years I did the whole suburban routine—clubs, babies, tennis, thrift shop, slaving away at school benefits. I was very busy and not at all unhappy.

It was just by chance a friend of mine was taking a course in art, and she didn't want to drive into the city alone, so I said I'd go with her. I got interested, and I was the kind of person who couldn't draw a straight line to save her life.

I just sort of slipped into taking more courses in education. There was an extension program, and I got the habit of enrolling. One afternoon I happened to be talking to one of my professors, and he asked me why I wasn't getting a degree. It was the second course I had taken with him, and I had done several papers and got A's. His courses were fabulous. I adored the classes. He suggested I think about a program of studies in his department. It had never occurred to me before. I was lucky to get accepted. They had hundreds of applicants for the program. I graduated with a bachelor's degree and went right on for a master's. I'm even thinking of going on for a doctorate.

In the beginning my husband was all for school. When he saw how much time it took and how interested I was, he did a complete turnabout. He became resentful. We had some terrible scenes. He wanted me to stop going. Said I was neglecting him and the children. That wasn't true at all. I was a better mother—off the kids' backs for a change; he couldn't see it that way. He wouldn't even talk about my work. I saw him getting shallower, while I felt my mind was developing by leaps and bounds.

I know the change in me bothered him. He was threatened. After all, he had married me as a very attractive unintellectual little girl. He was clearly the boss with a superior mind. He was caught up short when one day he discovered that his pretty, dependent little wife had changed. All the things that had counted before were gone.

I didn't neglect my appearance. I just wasn't as interested. I've loved every day since I made the discovery that I had brains in my head. I think I grew up in an era when being a sweet little wife was all that counted, and I learned to hide my talents. The discovery was a joy. My husband couldn't take it. Neither could I take him. I was the one who came right out and told him I wasn't going to stop, and if he wanted a divorce I wouldn't stop him. We didn't have babies to consider. The children are grown. I think in my case he was the one who was hurt by it all. He didn't want to go through with the divorce. I was the one who pushed, and I've never been sorry. I had to have my freedom.

Whatever the official and ostensible reasons for divorce, it obviously means much more than the end of a specific relationship. It entails a radical shift in an important part of a woman's identity. She can no longer anchor a significant part of her sense of self in her relationship with the person who has been her husband. It demands a change in her psychological as well as legal identity, and the psychological change often takes much longer than the legal process involved. There is a difference between legal and psychological divorce, and in some instances it may be some time after a legal divorce that a wife becomes psychologically divorced from her former husband. The echoes of lingering attachment are reflected in the comments of a forty-seven-year-old woman who had been divorced for nearly a year and a half.

I held up pretty well after the divorce. I have tried everything to hold on to him. He wouldn't go with me for marriage counseling. It was too late anyway. There was another woman. He got married a week after the divorce was final. I heard about it. There's always someone ready to tell you this kind of gossip. It doesn't matter, because sooner or later I had to face facts. He took the new wife on a three-month trip to Europe. Isn't that a twist? We never could get away for that length of time. It's always different with a second wife. They get the better deal.

I plugged along picking up the pieces of my life. It's funny, what really bothered me was hearing they had a baby less than a year after they were married. We had kids eighteen and twenty, and now he was the father of a baby—starting over again. I suppose I should have known this would happen, but it still made me uncomfortable. A friend asked me what was so shocking to me. After all, his second wife is a young girl. She wanted a child.

The night I heard the news I cried. It was a strange

feeling. The baby made the whole business terribly wrong, almost immoral. Of course, there was sex, but the baby made it seem twisted in my mind. The kids took it better than I. My daughter saw the baby and said it was adorable, looked exactly like her father. I find myself thinking about the baby, his new life, and our kids—myself. I know it will take time to get used to the idea my marriage is really over. I wonder if that's why the baby upset me the way it did.

The woman in her middle forties may also discover that divorce entails changes beyond those immediately and directly involved with her former husband. For most married couples, social life is organized in terms of marital units. One couple invites another couple to dinner, or to go out for a night on the town. The divorced woman is no longer a member of a functioning unit in the social framework within which she has lived. As a result, her entire pattern of social relationships may be disrupted, and the aspect of her identity that has been defined in terms of these social relationships inevitably must change.

A recently divorced woman in her middle forties described the experience.

I've learned the hard way that when I got a divorce I didn't only lose a husband, I lost a whole way of life. Not one of our old friends—married couples we knew for years—has ever bothered to call me. I was invited only once to a dinner party, and that was an experience. Women I had known for years behaved in a ridiculous way. I had the feeling they were scared to let me be in the room with their husbands alone. Maybe they were right. I was shocked when one of the men actually put his arm around me, and that squeeze didn't strike me as a brotherly kind of gesture. I resent all of this. The women think I'm out on the make, and the men have

some idea that now that I'm divorced I'd welcome any
bed partner.

That's what the score really is and that's what I mean
when I say a whole way of life is changed. You have to
make new friends. I find I'm out searching for a new
life with all the other divorcées. The singles don't want
you. You're competition. I get calls from widowers who
come right out and proposition me. They need a
housekeeper.

Divorced men are a different class, I'm convinced. I
know that my ex-husband is bombarded with invita-
tions. He is invited to all of our old friends' parties. A
married woman thinks twice before she invites an unat-
tached female; she jumps for men in the same position.
It hurts my pride. I have to admit, though, that when
I was married I wasn't any different. Every time I feel
bad, I ask myself about how many times I ever invited
a divorced woman to my house.

This change in the overall pattern of a divorced woman's
social interaction does not mean a change in individual
friendships. As a matter of fact, divorced or not, at this time
of stress, friendships with other women often take on greater
value than ever before.

A forty-six-year-old who was living through a period of
considerable marital stress talked about the importance of
her friendship with another woman.

I don't know what I would do without this friend. She
knows what I am going through. She either calls every
day or comes over. She's really saving me. Being able
to talk to someone made such a difference. She'd been
through it all. Her husband left her and five children
for nearly a year. She didn't break down, and at the
time no one, except me, knew how terrible life was for
her. He came back. There was a lot of pressure from

both sides of the family to get them back together again. They seem fairly happy now, though my friend said there are many times when it isn't easy. She hasn't let up once on her involvement with the children and the community. Even now she works part-time for a travel agency. She's a most unusual person.

Now I'm having my share of problems, and I would be lost if I didn't know that I could turn to her. She doesn't ask questions or anything like that. There's no probing for the gory details. I talk with her. I value her advice, even though I don't know if things will turn out as I hope, and I know she would like it to be that way for my sake.

Mothering

"The most draining and emotionally exhausting thing anyone can do."

During this period the children of the woman in her middle forties, usually middle-to-late adolescents, are living through their own normal problems of development, and the nature of their problems in interaction with her stresses adds another dimension to her personal crisis. Typically, the major developmental tasks of adolescents involve two interrelated issues: the establishment of their independence and the definition of their own identity. They want, and need, to be treated as individuals in their own right, without the protective parental guidance and limits of childhood. At the same time they also need to try out different possible identities, to experiment and test themselves in their search for a sense of self.

As anyone who has lived with an adolescent is well aware, it is generally not a quiet, smooth period of development. Rather, it's often fraught with emotional upheavals, periods of elation and then depression, leaps toward maturity and regressions to childhood. It is a period of normal inconsistency, of testing the limits both of oneself and of others, a time of frustration, conflict, and growth. Even under optimal conditions, with the best-integrated parents and children, this can be a time of considerable family strain.

The sources of stress derive not only from the individual psychological problems of those involved. They also reflect the interlocking educational, social, and economic systems of our society that may impose special pressures on the adolescent and his parents. This is particularly true in those families characterized by high achievement-orientation. Although many parents, as well as their children, vastly overrate the importance of factors such as academic achievement, getting into the so-called "right" schools and colleges, making the "right" decisions about one's future, being socially adjusted, it is nevertheless true that certain events during adolescence have some impact on the individual's future life. The long-range effects of these events are probably not nearly as great as some parents might feel, but they are important enough to provide a basis in objective reality for concern. A mother's worry about her children's achievement and adjustment is a widespread phenomenon.

Not at all unusual are the remarks of a forty-five-year-old woman about her adolescent son.

It bothers me to see my son not doing as well as he could in school. I've talked to him; my husband has talked to him. He isn't applying himself. I know he has the talents. He has a friend who I know hasn't one half the ability, and that child goes home with an excellent report card. The mother is a friend of mine, and even she has admitted that her son isn't a real student. She's amazed how well he does. I wish we could be the kind of parents who could sit back and let a child just go along at his own pace. We can't. I wonder if any parent can just sit and watch their child go down the drain because of plain laziness. I think we're absolutely right in keeping after him. Someday he'll appreciate what we're doing.

This concern with a child's achievement and status is intensified when parents view their child's adolescence as an opportunity to make up for their own past frustrations. In the words of a woman in her middle forties talking about her children, "You do live partly in your children's accomplishments."

I can't blame myself for wanting my kids to go to better schools, do more with their lives than me or my husband. I think that's only natural. My parents came to this country without a dime to their names. They made their way, and they wanted a better life for their children. I suppose we're doing the same thing to our kids. It's harder on kids today than it was for us, I suppose. For my parents a college education was a goal in itself.

Now the kids have many more options. College isn't enough. They're pushed on to graduate schools. Everything is bigger and much more. I wonder if that's why lots of kids of this generation are throwing over everything. In a way, I don't blame them.

I don't see how it could be different. You do live partly in your children's accomplishments. There's some borrowed glory, and I don't care who you are. I know my husband was out with our son's team. My husband never made any high school or college team. When our son was elected captain, we tried not to make a fuss over him, and yet it was kind of nice. We would only be lying if we didn't say we felt good. It's been the same with other things in which any one of the children did exceedingly well. At forty-seven you can't be captain. You get a second chance at going around adolescence through your children.

Sometimes, a mother may recognize her adolescent children's need for independence, their need to make their own decisions, live their own lives, even make their own mistakes. Yet, her emphatic involvement with her children at this point may be so great that, even with her awareness, she cannot control her behavior.

A forty-six-year-old woman was well aware of her daughter's need for independence, but as the following remarks clearly indicate, this woman could not inhibit her active concern.

I can't understand why my daughter isn't more popular. She's a very pretty girl, has a lovely figure, is bright, intelligent, does so many things—and she's never asked out. It's breaking my heart to see her on a Saturday night sitting in her room.

I can't understand boys nowadays. I think it's because she won't sleep around. Her friends do. She's told me, and I've talked to other women, and I know what's going on. My husband isn't at all concerned. I can't talk with him about the subject. He says if I make an issue of it she'll really have a problem. I know I should let her be. The time will come, and she will have her turn. Right now I feel guilty when my husband and I go out, and she's sitting home alone or perhaps has a girl friend over to spend the evening.

Intellectually I know a child has to have her own life, develop at her own pace. But when you're a mother and you sit on the sidelines, there are times when your heart breaks. Many a time I have this feeling I'm living through her adolescence. When something happens to your child or your child is unhappy it's far worse than when it happens to you. With me even when my outside world, my job, my work are all going well, if the world's not right for my child, I am broken up inside.

Sometimes I have this feeling that being the right kind of parent is the most draining and emotionally exhausting thing anyone can do. I'd give a lot sometime to say to myself—and really mean what I say—that I don't care at all. "The children have their own lives and have to live their own lives. I shouldn't be at all interested in what happens to them." I don't believe there is a parent living today who can say and believe this. They're only kidding themselves.

Parental interest is not itself the issue—adolescents need and want it. The conflict develops when this interest is manifested in behaviors that children see as nagging, overprotection, placing unreasonable limits on them, intruding on their personal lives. Consider, for example, the comments made by a fifteen-year-old boy about his middle-forties mother.

My mother bugs me—a lot sometimes. Don't misunderstand me, we get along fine; it's just that—well, like when I'm on the phone with a friend she always seems to have "something" to do in the same room. Sometimes she just stands there listening. That gets me—I mean, I don't try to listen to her conversations with *her friends.* One thing for sure, she's not going to be able to do that for her whole life.

Another thing, like the times when Lisa comes over and I can't get within three feet of her without Mom bursting into my room asking me some crazy question like "What did you do with my toenail clippers?"

Could you imagine what hell I'd get if I burst into my parents' room at eleven at night yelling "What did you do with my football?"

Dates, and especially first dates, are the worst. Right down the line: "What did you do?" "What does she look like?" "Are her parents nice?" "I'll bet she didn't even say thank you."

I sort of feel like climbing into a hole every time I'm doing something that's not quite right in her eyes or not doing something that supposedly I should be. Then it's a battle because I never do certain things because she nags me about them. Doesn't she have her own life to worry about?

A mid-forties mother is most likely to consider her parental concern not only normal, but an imperative part of her role as mother. Nevertheless, this concern leads her into clashes with her children that can be frighteningly explosive, and perhaps most disturbing of all, can result in a serious breakdown of communication. She is sometimes torn between her desire to intervene and her fear of antagonizing her children, a situation that is bound to leave her anxious and frustrated.

This sense of frustration is reflected in the remarks of a forty-seven-year-old woman whose son, from her point of view, was inevitably heading for trouble.

It kills me to stand by knowing sometimes he's bound to get hurt, knowing what's going to happen, and my hands are tied. I've tried talking to him. It doesn't do any good. If anything, it's made matters worse. He's a beautiful kid. We couldn't ask for anything more. He did well in school. Everything was going right for him, and then he met this woman several years older than he is.

She has two children, illegitimate. She wouldn't give

them up for adoption. She latched on to our son. At twenty he's a father—not really, but treats the children as if he were the father. Every time those kids call him "Daddy" our hearts could break. The girl wants to get married. How is he going to support her? He can't go on to school and support a wife and children that aren't even his.

We started out screaming about it. That only made him resentful—he wouldn't have anything to do with us for a while. Then we tried to reason with him. If he'd only wait. Give the relationship time. Not rush into something that might ruin his whole life. The girl is wrong for him. She's five years older than he is. The father of the children wasn't the first man she lived with. She's not for him. She has him crawling to her, and we can't understand what's happened to him. All I do is touch on the subject, and there's an explosion in the house. I know I can't live his life for him. He's not a child. He's an adult. Standing by watching him being destroyed has taken the heart our of our lives.

If she has also been undergoing a period of strain in her relationship with her husband, the conflicts with her children may be experienced as even more stressful. In their marital battles, it is not at all unlikely that her husband has blamed her for the problems they have had with their children, thus adding a degree of guilt to a growing emotional burden.

It is precisely at this time in her own development that she is likely to feel an especially strong need to be needed —a need that is frustrated by her husband's withdrawal and rejection and her children's striving for independence. She offers love, support, guidance, help to others—and the significant people in her life counter with hostility and the desire to escape from her nurturing.

Children's sexual drives certainly don't begin in adolescence, but the acquisition of adult sexual characteristics is obviously an important part of adolescent development. For most parents this is not a major issue. It is one more step in their children's history of growth. In fact, it may be viewed, at least at a conscious level, in a positive light as a sign of their children's healthy and normal development.

However, for the middle-forties mother, this reaction, particularly in relation to her daughter, is sometimes accompanied by less positive feelings. A mother is usually not aware of the motives underlying her apprehensiveness and anxiety, and for the most part these feelings are successfully repressed. Nevertheless, they may be shown in overconcern about her daughter's real or imagined sexual behavior, or as in the following instance, about the child's physical development.

I don't know what to do about my daughter. I've tried to talk to her, and it doesn't do any good. This past year she developed a large bosom. After a fight, I finally got her to wear a bra. She wants to wear body shirts. She looks awful in clothes like that. She seems completely unaware of her appearance. Comments of her brothers make no impression. She goes her own way.

My husband sees nothing wrong. He told me if we keep making a point of it she'll become self-conscious. His attitude is if she's got it, flaunt it. It bothers me terribly his saying something like this about his own daughter. His attitude is very different from mine.

I know boys; eventually she's going to get hurt by the things they'll say. It's only for her sake that I'm concerned. My husband insists she'd probably feel worse if she were flat-chested. I don't agree with him. That's a male point of view.

Sometimes she comes down to the dinner table, and

I could die. The other evening she sat there without a bra in one of the scoop-necked cotton shirts the girls wear nowadays, and I finally exploded. I told her either she had to dress decently or she could eat alone. She burst out crying, and my husband and I had a terrible argument.

There are two factors that appear to be fairly common when her adolescent's sexual development is a major problem for the middle-forties mother. In some cases sexual characteristics and behaviors symbolize the child's general maturation, and sexuality may become the central issue around which battles of independence are fought. In addition, as a mother feels herself growing older and perhaps sexually less desirable, she may feel, almost always at an unconscious level, some pangs of jealousy toward a daughter growing sexually more attractive.

It would be absurd to conclude that jealousy is a primary source of motivation in a mother's overall reaction to her daughter. Much stronger are the love and affection, pride and happiness associated with her child's normal development. Nevertheless, when such envy is felt, it may add considerably to the stress of the middle forties.

Eventually, the middle-forties mother will realize that the kids are no longer kids, as shown in the observations of a forty-six-year-old woman.

You can't help it if you're a mother thinking of your kids as babies—and that has nothing to do with being in diapers. Then one day it hits you that they're not babies. They've grown up. You're not the center of their world. They don't come to you any more. My son has a steady girl friend; my daughter has a steady boy friend. I'm out of the picture, and the fact they've both grown up has sneaked up on me without my even knowing it was happening. When that day came, that was the day I felt old.

To the mid-forties mother the realization that "the kids are no longer kids" may be a major sign of her own aging. She is already sensitized to growing older, and now she must face the fact that she is no longer the mother of young children; she is the mother of people who are nearly adults. In addition, there is the recognition that her role as mother must undergo a significant change. The child-rearing behaviors, the protective attitudes that may have defined her role as mother for almost two decades are now clearly inappropriate. They are not only inappropriate, they are sorely resented and rejected by her children. The middle-forties woman may therefore face a sharp discontinuity in what is expected and wanted from her in her role as mother, adding another source of stress to her sense of identity.

The Children Leave

"I've kept their rooms the same."

The final step in this sequence comes when the children leave home. For some it may just involve a psychological withdrawal; the children may still be physically present, but they gradually withdraw from the kind of parent-child interactions that once characterized family life. They become much more concerned about maintaining their own privacy, and their lives become increasingly focused on the world of their peers. If the child remains in the family home at this time, it may seem as if a stranger has moved in—at best, a courteous stranger who keeps to himself; at worst, a sullen, angry stranger who lives as if he were in a state of siege surrounded by enemies. This sense of hostile siege is conveyed by the remarks of a nineteen-year-old currently living at home.

If I had money I'd get out. I hate being dependent on them. Screw them. I live in the house. I have my own room, and they don't come in. I told them I'll leave. Meanwhile what I do in the room and how I keep it is my business. If they say one more word I'm getting out. They don't want me to go. My mother goes down on her knees and cries. I got a few more months of school and I graduate. I'll be getting out, and I can't wait for the day. I've never liked my father. He doesn't respect me. I know that—and fuck him.

My mother—she's weak; she cries; she tiptoes around the family. I can't stand that. I think she's nuts to take that crap from my father. She keeps crying to me that they tried hard with me. I suppose they did what they could when I was a little kid. They have no feeling for me now as a person. There's a big wall between us. They don't know me—inside me. They don't understand. Her crying about my being her son and she loves me turns me off. I told her that. My father—I've had it up to here with his talks. "Shove it," I told him the last time. "Let me alone."

The more obvious break comes, of course, when the children physically leave home. This changes the outward pattern of family living, but in fact may be easier to adjust to than the uneasy atmosphere that prevails when the child leaves only psychologically. In any event, when her child moves out, there comes an important and necessary change in a mother's role.

The last child left home for college. I told my husband that this was the end of our being together as a family. The children don't come home again to stay, once they go off to college. You pretend they're not leaving. I've kept their rooms the same. Scrapbooks, records, books are all on the shelves.

The other day I was cleaning the shelves, and I dropped one of the model airplanes, and a wing fell off. I spent an hour trying to glue pieces back together. My son hasn't looked at that airplane in years, and I'm sure he'll never want it. Yet I can't bring myself to throw it in the garbage.

When children leave home, it's a real change in life. It hits you how much of your world has revolved around them. God knows, there were times I hated the life and would say to myself if only I could have a whole day without any lists, meals to prepare, laundry. And then the day comes, and they're not around, and I miss them.

It takes adjusting, more so than I ever realized, now that the last child is out of the house. We're thinking of moving. We know the place is too big for the two of us. It's a waste to have three empty bedrooms. I told my husband we started out twenty-four years ago in a four-room apartment, and twenty-four years later we belong right back where we started from. We should make the move because it's silly to have all this money tied up in a house we don't need.

My husband isn't as upset as I am. He wants all the changes and tells me it will be good for us. It isn't that he doesn't love the kids, but for him it is different. His work is a big part of his life. With me, it was the other way around. The children and the house were the main things; everything else I did was extra.

Worries About Parents

"They were like my kids and I was their parent."

As a woman moves through the fifth decade of life, her parents are likely to be faced with the problems of old age. There may be illness, financial insecurity, loneliness, emotional distress—a wide range of problems that the elderly encounter.

Both men and women in their forties meet these problems, and both men and women must deal with their responsibilities to their parents. Sons are no less generous than daughters in fulfilling these responsibilities. Nevertheless, for one reason or another, in our society, the major emotional burden of this stage seems to be assumed by the daughters of aged parents. Therefore, in addition to other concerns about herself, the problems of her parents may be a significant source of stress, as in the case of this forty-six-year-old woman.

> When the good days come I have this feeling I want to hold on to them, make time stop. My philosophy is take any happiness you have in twenty-four hours and hold on. God knows, there are enough problems around the corner. I guess I'm feeling low at the moment mostly because of my parents. They're both getting older. I don't want to face it. They've always been very full of life, and I can see them slowing down, and I'm bothered when they bring up the subject. I get knots and won't let them talk about how they feel.
>
> My father has started talking about the "great beyond," and Mother starts in with "after I'm gone." I hate thinking about it. It doesn't do me any good, and

I don't think it helps them. They've been very ill, and it's fallen on my shoulders.

I think that's what makes a woman feel old. When you're in your thirties, parents are younger; family problems don't seem to be earth-shaking. You move a few years; the kids are older, parents are older, and our problems are bigger, coping becomes a struggle.

With my parents, it's been up to me to handle it. I don't fault my brothers. They are concerned, but let's face it: my mother simply can't sit down with a son and cry. He can't take tears. It's not that I'm comfortable seeing her cry, but I understand and can accept it better, or at least pretend that I do. All I know is she comes to me. It isn't that she's complaining; she's worried and I'm worried, too, for her. I think about them a lot, and and there's nothing much I can do. At times, I want to run and hide ostrichlike—shut it all out, and other times I'm frantically calling and visiting and doing what I can.

Concerns about her parents add to the general level of stress the middle-forties woman is experiencing at this time. They may also carry a special psychological meaning for her. At a time of stress it is normal and healthy to share your fears and worries with those closest to you, and the woman in her middle forties may very well feel the need to talk about her own problems with her parents. A forty-four-year-old woman described this feeling.

Sometimes I feel I could go out of my mind listening to problems. The kids want to talk to me. They've got worries. My husband has his concerns. Mothers aren't supposed to worry; their job is to listen to everybody else. I need someone to talk to, and I don't mean an analyst's couch; I mean "backyard fence" talk.

When the children were young, it was easier. I'd sit in the park with other mothers. We'd talk and listen to each other, and we felt better because we knew everyone was in the same boat. Now it's not the same. The children are big; I'm not out in the park. Everyone is busy. You just don't sit down with a group and have a "busy bee" club meeting. I'm working, too. Other women are working. A lot of our social relationships are very superficial. We all put up good fronts. You don't let your hair down at a cocktail party.

And yet there are times when I want someone to talk to. I feel like jumping back in time and wanting to sit down and tell someone—my mother—how I feel. I did this. I surprised myself. There was a lot of difficulty in the house—and I was having a hard time pulling myself together. I couldn't talk to my husband. He was upset.

I got on the phone and called my mother. I felt very foolish in a way, embarrassed—forty-four years old and still calling my mother for advice. I was taken back to college days when I'd call home desperately from a hall telephone. I don't even think she heard me, but when I hung up I felt drained, relieved, a lot better. Maybe there are moments when all of us have to behave like kids, regardless of how old we are.

There is nothing wrong or unusual about the impulse, at any age, to share personal concerns with the people who are closest to you. But if the parents of the woman in her middle forties are facing difficulties of their own, she probably feels that they cannot be expected to share her problems as they might have in the past. Thus, a major source of emotional support may no longer be available to her.

Another, somewhat more subtle, issue is even more directly related to the particular problems of aging being faced by the woman in her forties. It involves the psychological implications of assuming a "care-taking" role in relation to her own parents. This often involves a significant shift in her role as daughter, a shift reflected in the comments of a forty-seven-year-old woman who discussed the need to care for her parents.

Both my parents became ill this past year. My mother had a heart attack; my father fell and fractured his hip. When this happened, the two of them fell apart. They're in their late seventies, and not being able to get around and do what they've always done nearly killed them more than having to be hospitalized.

They're home now. I don't know what to do. They live in the country, and I haven't been able to find anyone to stay with them. It's such a twist. All their lives, they were the support for their children. I know myself I always went out to their place to unwind. Mother is a very easy person to be around. Her whole life is involved with her children, my dad, the house. She's the kind of woman people turn to with problems. I am the first to admit that she is the one I always go to when I have a worry. Now she called me and tried not to cry. I know, though, she's very upset. She has started asking me what to do, how she can handle Dad, who gets depressed.

It makes me feel very strange her turning to me like this when she was the one I turned to. I've been out every week, and I think I'm going to have to insist they come stay with us until they're back on their feet again. When I told her, I expected her to argue and Dad to throw a fit. Neither said a word. They sat there—the two of them—and said if I thought it was best, then they'd come for a while. They didn't want to cause trouble; yet they knew they couldn't just stumble along in poor health alone out there.

I felt torn inside having Mom ask me what she should bring and what to do about closing the house, the mail, her garden. Here I was in her role. I felt as if I aged years in minutes. I had to fight back tears. They were like my kids, and I was the parent. I know they'll get better. It's interesting, though, because while I am telling them what to do, I feel very much an adult. It's as if my days of being the daughter going to them for help are over. I don't know why I am upset at this the way I am.

Throughout her adult life, a large part of the identity of the woman who is now in her middle forties has been anchored in her relationships with other people—her husband, her children, her parents. At this stage, external forces operate to disrupt these relationships. By virtue of her husband's own developmental crisis, her role as wife may be threatened; as a consequence of her children's growing maturity, her role as mother inevitably shifts; and as a result of the normal problems of aging met by her parents, her role as daughter must undergo significant change.

In addition, her emotional reactions to one source of threat and change interact with and influence her reactions to other problems. For example, the difficulties she encounters in relationship to her husband are inextricably bound up with her emotional reactions to the problems she faces with her children. We do not live in emotion-tight compartments; the stresses of one area of life spill over and influence our reactions in other areas. The middle-forties woman is thus caught in a web of relationships in the process of change, relationships that have in the past served to define major aspects of her personality. As a result, she is no longer sure of her psychological self. She is a woman in crisis, anxious, angry, confused—threatened by a loss of her own identity.

Juggling Career and Family

"My life is a struggle in a sinking boat."

A woman who has pursued a career and whose identity has not been anchored primarily in the family probably encounters less threat to her identity at this stage of life. A central aspect of the career woman's self is defined by interests that are not directly involved in the strains of family interactions. In a difficult time of interpersonal changes, the woman in her middle forties who is working can draw strength from a portion of her life that is relatively independent of these specific stresses, and thus face the vicissitudes of this period with a certain degree of equanimity.

If she has remained single, loneliness continues to be a potential problem. She may deal with this issue by increasing the extent of her social activities, becoming more involved with friends and relatives. For example, she may invest a good deal of herself—her time, energy, interest, and love—in developing relationships with nieces and nephews, the children of friends or other members of her family. Another important avenue of personal satisfaction involves renewed dedication to her career, the rewards stemming not only from professional advancement but also from the interpersonal relationships entailed in her work. The chief ad-

ministrator of a hospital described the director of nurses, a
single woman in her middle forties.

I'm not overstating the case when I say that without
her the place would fall apart. She's been here twenty-
five years. I came five years ago, and I wonder if I'll last
that long, with some of the problems we face around
here. We're a big institution. She has over a thousand
staff to worry about. We run the gamut—well-trained
to poorly trained. It's not easy to get a top-notch nursing staff together, and that's what you need to carry the
patient load we've got.

She's in that office at seven in the morning. I go
home at six. She's still here. Has an apartment over in
the nurses' residence. I can't tell you how many times
I hear the same story—she's been back here in the
evenings covering if there's an emergency. The place
is her life. There's no doubt about it. She handles that
staff with a kid glove and iron hand. That's what's
needed. There's not a person around who doesn't respect her.

You take the medical staff. They'll tell everyone off,
pull rank. With her, she says one word, and they take
two steps backwards. Don't misunderstand me.
They're not afraid of her in that sense. They know she
knows her business. They respect her. I've seen the
chief of surgery call her in and ask her what she
thinks before he goes ahead and makes some kind of
procedural change on the floor. You've got to hand it
to a woman like that.

She has her off moments like any of us. There's no
doubt about it, though, she cares about the patients,
and there isn't a thing she wouldn't do for a staff
member. If she thinks some nurse is in the right she'll
go all out.

She's a nice-looking woman. I wonder why she never

got married. Caught up in her work, I guess. She certainly has lots of friends here at the hospital, and I know she's involved with her nieces. We had two of them here as students in the nursing school. I know they're close to her. When they graduated, she told me she gave them each a trip to Europe as a present. She said they were going to spend many a day with the pain and suffering of others and deserved a fling before they started to work.

If the middle-forties woman has family responsibilities in addition to her work, she continues to face the same kinds of concerns she has probably had throughout the years of working and raising a family, as reflected in the remarks of a forty-five-year-old business woman.

I don't care who she is. Any woman who has children and a full-time job has worries a man never has. It just isn't the same for a woman as a man. It's easier now for me because the kids are fifteen and sixteen, but there were many times those first years when working and managing a house was a nightmare. I still cringe at some of the memories.

One time we had a housekeeper who we thought was a jewel. I thought she was fabulous with the kids, better than I was. One day at work I get a call from an absolute stranger who lived in the building. She told me she found the kids sitting outside. Neither had shoes on, and it was winter. She went back to the apartment with them; the door was wide open and the "jewel" was in the kitchen with an empty bottle of Scotch.

There was another time when I couldn't get decent regular help, and I went out of my mind juggling a schedule. My husband did try to help. I can't blame him, but he couldn't stay away from some of the conferences out of town. It all fell on my shoulders.

I hear young couples now telling me how they are going to make sure they divide the responsibilities of kids. That's fine, if both partners have the kinds of jobs that allow them alternate times off. The crises in our lives have always come when both of us have tight schedules, and it's left up to me to muddle through problems at home.

People you hire are a mixed bag. Some are going to be good; others are going to walk out and leave the kids the minute your back is turned. Maybe some of these couples will be lucky. They'll have some kind of Mary Poppins come into their houses when the kids are born and stay devoted until the kids go away to college. No one I know has that kind of luck.

I've heard worse horror stories than mine. A friend came home and found her eighteen-month-old had been strapped in a highchair all day. The child was hysterical. Hadn't been changed once. She fired the girl and started over again with agencies.

Certainly there are millions of times when all goes smoothly, though you're never free from a nagging concern. Even now I find myself looking at the clock about three-thirty, wondering if they got home O.K., and if the girl showed up. She only comes half-days. Stays through supper. There's always a thread of guilt troubling a woman. I don't think men feel this. Their attitude is like my husband's. Kids will survive and be better off for their independence. He may be right. As far as I am concerned, I never have a complete sense of security and freedom.

When her children are living through the problems of adolescence, the middle-forties mother may feel they need extra time and attention from her—though her children themselves may very well disagree with this view. In any event, the conflict she feels between the demands of her work and the demands of her family may become even more intense at this time, with resultant guilt feelings about neglecting her children or neglecting her work. Even if she were free of all job demands, she probably couldn't do much to ease her children's normal strains through their adolescence. Regardless of this, however, the mid-forties career mother may feel uncomfortable about not having as much time and energy available for her children as she might have if she were not working. A forty-six-year-old woman working in public relations expressed these feelings.

I want to laugh every time I read some magazine article about a career woman who says it doesn't matter the amount of time she spends with her children that counts, it's the quality. Maybe these women have some special secret formula. I wish they'd tell me. I would love to know how I can give quality after a long demanding day at the office. Most of the time after work I want a hot shower, a cocktail, and a good book. The last thing I want is children demanding attention. I don't have the energy, and I don't want to listen to more problems. I can't sit down and worry about who lost a ball-point pen. I'm not up to tutoring fifth-grade math, which I am not sure of anyhow.

My work is high-pressured. Many an evening I come home with a briefcase of work. My husband does, too. I've noticed as the children get older, they want more time. They get out of school at three, and I don't get home until six or later if I have a board meeting. They can't wait to pounce on me.

It was much easier to work when they were small. The girl took them out in the afternoon, and they were ready to go to bed after dinner. Now some days they want to talk, talk, talk. And after a day of talk I want silence. I do suffer guilt. The times I've turned them off are times that I get up the next day with a headache.

I won't give up my career, and there are moments I wonder if having them was a mistake. Anyhow, there's not much I can do about that now. I think they're at that age, they need a lot of time, and I know it will get easier again. Right now it's very tiring. I feel exhausted, holding down two jobs—a full-time professional career and the family.

Although the conflict between these two jobs is not unique to the middle-forties professional, the feelings of strain may be especially strong at this time, partly because of the increased demands of her work. The progress of her career may have been hampered by bias against women, and chances are that she has advanced more slowly than some of her male colleagues. It is more than likely that as she has moved up the ladder of status and power, each successive step has been more difficult. At this stage, she may be working with greater involvement than ever, striving to take that next important step that could mean reaching a long-range goal—and it is often just at this point that her family begins to make even greater demands on her time and energy. A forty-seven-year-old advertising executive who had recently started the most important project in her career described the conflicts she faced.

I honestly believe the enviable difference between men and women is men can compartmentalize their lives. It's very different for women. I look at myself. I've reached a point in my career that I'm almost at the top —a stone's throw away from everything I've worked for these past years. And it can all crash down, not because of my not being able to handle the work. I could accept that. I could say to myself I wasn't good enough or male chauvinism stopped me, but that isn't what's holding me down. My husband is picking at me. His life is screwed up. He accuses me, resents me. I can feel it.

Little comments he makes. He's going through some sort of madness. If he were a woman, I'd say he was reaching menopause.

And then, the children. We never had problems with them. Now, as if to spite my success, they decide it's time to try the whole adolescent bit—drugs, sex, drinking. I know they'll come out of it all right, but at this moment I feel I'm walking on glass.

The older one took the car out after he had a breakup with his girl friend. He had something to drink, drove it a hundred miles an hour and crashed into a tree. He's alive—came out practically unscratched. No one—the police, anyone who saw that car—can understand how he escaped with a few scratches. At work I shudder when the telephone rings. What next?

Last summer we rented a sailboat, and it was a rough day. Wave after wave kept hitting the side of the boat. That's how I feel. I just have one wave slap at me before another rolls in, and that day in the boat I worried because I thought we would all be washed over the side. That's how it is now. My life is like a struggle with a sinking boat.

A special problem may arise at this time if a woman's career becomes more successful than her husband's. This does not always cause marital difficulties, but at a stage when the husband is particularly sensitive about his own advancement, whatever rivalry has been implicit in their relationship is likely to become more intense. A forty-seven-year-old business woman discussed her own situation in terms of this issue.

I have a job that pays more and has more status than my husband's. It just happened that way. I started back to work in a firm that needed to promote women because of government contracts. I was available. The-right-time, the-right-place sort of thing. It bothered him. He'll make comments to me. It was O.K. for me to work and to bring home money. That was fine. Only when I moved up did he get resentful. He'll call me the boss-lady, or he'll say something like we can use his check for pin money.

It makes me very unhappy. When he made more than I did, I never said anything. It didn't occur to me to be bothered. I wasn't raised as a woman's lib girl, but I believe in it all now. Why shouldn't I make good money? Why shouldn't I have a title that counts in the office? What no one talks about is what are you going to do about the man in your life who sees himself slipping the other way while you move up. It's very difficult. I know that if it comes to choosing between the career I have and him, I'm going to choose him. I don't see any other way out.

The middle-forties woman engaged in a career thus has certain advantages as well as certain problems. Because of her involvement in activities outside the family, she may be less disturbed by the disruption of relationships with significant others. Her sense of self-worth is not entirely dependent on her roles as wife, mother, daughter; therefore, threats to her functioning in these roles may not be felt as strongly. At the same time, however, she may experience the added stress of feeling torn between the heightened demands made on her both at work and at home.

Aging

"I haven't enough energy to stay awake."

Because the process of physical aging is often exacerbated by the psychological tension associated with it, the normal aches and pains that come as one grows older tend to add to the overall stress experienced in the middle forties, as in the case of a forty-six-year-old woman suffering from recurrent back pains.

Not one doctor can tell me what's wrong. One has said a pinched nerve, another wants me to have an operation for a disk. I can't keep any of the diagnoses straight at this point. All I know is that the pain is excruciating. It starts up here near my shoulder and moves along my back. I have a neck collar on now, and it's some relief. But I wonder if it is helping me. The minute I take it off I feel paralyzed. There are days when I'm flat on my back in bed. I can't read, I can't move. Getting dressed is an effort. They have me on some kind of painkiller and tranquilizer now, but I hate them. I feel listless with the medication. I haven't enough energy to stay awake. I know it's hard for my husband. I can't do things around the house; meals have been makeshift. In a way I guess it hasn't hurt him as much as I thought. He has lost about twenty-five pounds and is still going. He took the kids on a camping trip to give me some rest, and I was surprised when they came back. He didn't look much older than our son who is in college.

Money Worries

"I feel I'm living under the shadow of the dollar sign."

When she is in her middle forties, a woman is probably enjoying an income that is higher than ever before. However, spending may outrun income at a pace even exceeding that of previous years. College tuition, medical expenses, house repairs—there sometimes seems to be an endless stream of mounting bills. At the same time, there are concerns about the future, and the woman in her middle forties may feel that she is on a treadmill of economic worries.

It is interesting that the absolute amount of income—short of the extremes of wealth and poverty—doesn't seem to make a great deal of difference in the degree of economic concern the middle-forties woman is likely to feel, though with higher income, the nature of the worries may be different. A forty-six-year-old woman living in a prosperous suburban area talked about her financial worries.

The other day I read an article about a group of young people who formed a commune. None of the members can have money. Everything is supplied by the commune. I thought to myself at the time, those kids aren't so crazy. There are times I wish I were in that situation. It's gotten terrible. I worry about money constantly. I can't talk about the subject with my husband. He makes a very good living. I have a part-time job. If you look at our income on paper, you would say we have a vice! There has to be some reason we're in debt up to our necks. The fact is, we haven't any extra money and we haven't any vices. We don't go out. We don't drink; we gave up cigarettes. I don't buy anything for myself, except if it's hanging on a sales rack. I'll tell you where the money is going. You have kids, and in this age it costs a fortune. They want lessons, and I want them to have lessons. One kid takes the guitar; another wants voice lessons; my daughter wants to study ballet. Every time I turn around I'm paying another teacher.

I suppose part of it is my fault. I should tell each of them to buy an instruction book and teach themselves. If one wants a new dress she has to earn the money. I don't know what's right or wrong. They are under pressure from their friends. I know that. Where do you draw the line? On the one hand you want them to have friends, but if all their friends are going to a party, do you say no? I tried that tactic. I told my son he should never follow the herd. He was to be independent. If all the boys went skiing for a weekend and he didn't have the money, he could do something else. Let me tell you how independence worked in our society. He stayed by himself, didn't do what the other kids did, and the school guidance counselor called me in and told me my son had to learn how to get along with his peers. He wasn't fitting in with the group. I wish I had an answer. I haven't, and I worry will we have enough to educate him.

What if something happens to my husband? We're not getting younger. We have to think of money for retirement. That time is coming quicker than we realize. Sometimes I go to bed wishing I could turn the clock backwards. When we were married we didn't have these worries. We didn't have children. Just the two of us. It was better even when they were babies. Only now when they're older and we're older, I feel I'm living under the shadow of the dollar sign.

The Shaken Self

"I wanted to scream."

Beset as she is by difficulties in her changing relationships with her husband, her children, and her parents, stressed by frustrations in her career, plagued by physical aches and pains, and preoccupied with economic worries, the sense of identity of the woman in her middle forties is understandably shaken. She may feel bewildered, confused, unsure. Life seems to be one problem after another, all adding up to meaningless drudgery. Sometimes in the face of major trauma, the woman in her middle forties focuses on the trivia of her life, as in the case of this forty-six-year-old woman.

It hit me quite suddenly—the feeling, I mean, of what my life added up to. I can remember exactly. I was having a second cup of coffee. Kids had gone off to school; my husband left for work. I tell you, my hands were shaking; I wanted to scream. One more set of breakfast dishes to clean up; one more dinner to worry about; one more bed to make; one more load of laundry. I'd had it, I tell you. I wanted to scream. At that moment if someone had just given me a one-way ticket anywhere I would have jumped. Slammed the door on the whole routine.

My husband says to me he helps. Who does the cleaning up after supper, he tells me. Well, bully for him. He puts a few dishes in the dishwasher. The kids are supposed to help. Will you tell me why a child fifteen years old won't screw on the top of a catsup bottle after I remind him a hundred times? I could do without my husband cleaning up. All it means is I have to go back and throw cleanser into the sink to get out stains. He won't take a sponge and scrub stains.

You know what really gets to me? Socks! Will you please tell me why children and one adult male can't stop turning socks inside out and throwing them into the laundry? For eighteen years I've turned socks inside out and matched pairs. Underwear the same. Inside out. Shirts inside out and dumped into the laundry. That's maybe the story of my life—inside out and backwards.

The woman in her middle forties sometimes feels that her problems will never end. Yet as time goes on, the external pressures of everyday living are reduced; the strain is eased. Life begins to regain some of the stability of earlier years, and with the movement from the middle to the late forties, there begins a crucial period of reintegration and psychological growth.

Although the gains of this stage are often not fully consolidated until sometime after the decade of the forties, the personality change and restructuring initiated in the late forties are particularly important. It is during this period that certain earlier conflicts are resolved, and a stage of significantly enhanced personal fulfillment may be achieved.

Two major themes characterize the psychological growth of the woman in her late forties. First, having lived through the stress of the middle forties, she is motivated, in part, by a search for security. It is not primarily financial or other-directed security; rather, it is a deeper, more fundamental sense of personal value that she seeks. She becomes less concerned with social relationships as a means of achieving status. She becomes less interested in physical appearance for the sake of pleasing and attracting others. These and other aspects of her life come to be viewed in a new light that emphasizes the inner-directed quality of experience.

Closely related to this shift in the pattern of her motivation and values is a gradual increase in individuation, independence, self-assertiveness. Up to this point her identity has been defined largely in terms of her roles with significant others. Indeed, it was principally the disturbances in these relationships that led to the crisis of identity in the middle forties. For the late-forties woman, these relationships retain their importance; but, having survived the stresses of recent years, she discovers in herself a degree of ego strength that she was unaware of before. She has learned that she can live through the threat of rejection by her husband—and emerge a psychologically integrated person. She has found that she can suffer the trials of her children's adolescent maturation—and remain a worthwhile human being in her own right. She has discovered that she can take on the responsibility of caring for aging parents—and as a result become a stronger, more effective adult. This self-discovery is the basis of reintegrating her sense of personal identity.

None of this happens overnight. A woman in her late forties does not decide at one particular point that she is a stronger person and then display a dramatic burst of psychological development. Instead, it is a gradual process, usually extending into the fifties. As part of her day-to-day living, she slowly discovers her self— a self in the process of change and growth.

late forties

The Quality of Marriage

*"At least I know even though storms come,
they pass."*

During the crisis of the middle forties, marital strain may
become so great that divorce is considered. If the couple
successfully negotiates this period, however, they often become closer than ever before. Husband and wife have lived
together through a period of intense stress, and the sharing
of this experience in and of itself seems to lead to a strength-
ening of the bond between them, as indicated by a woman
in her late forties.

There was a time when fights we had left me drained.
I didn't think I could survive. He would get angry, and
I'd cry. I could have committed suicide or murder. It
was a toss-up between the two. Now it isn't all peace
and light, believe me. At least I know even though
storms come, they pass. What's more, they don't last
as long. They're more like sun showers than tornadoes.
What a relief.

I know, too, even though we may have our differences and battle them out, there's a core between us
all these surface upsets can't touch. I'm not going to
leave him. He's not going to leave me. No one is going
to kill the other. We'll manage. The odd part of it is
that as time goes on there are fewer upsets. Both of us

are trying, I'm sure. We seem to be able to step back a bit and sometimes we even laugh ourselves out of situations we used to look at as if they were the end of the world.

As a consequence of living through the stresses of the middle forties, other changes also occur in a woman's relationship with her husband. Among the most important of these is her perception of him and his own self-perception in relation to his wife. Even though people may live together intimately for many years, certain culturally derived myths are likely to influence their perceptions of each other. In the American culture, the stereotyped view of the man as the stronger, more independent, and more active member of a marital relationship often subtly influences a wife's perception of her husband. Sometimes, regardless of his actual behavior, she may need, or want, to see him in this way; and his own needs are quite likely to be congruent with this stereotype.

The late-forties wife has been faced with the realities of her husband as a human being—his weaknesses, fears, his need for her support and reassurance. Like every other mature human being, he is inevitably dependent on others, and he may finally recognize and accept the reality of this dependency. From this point of view, then, the marital relationship may become more realistic and human. This kind of change was described by a woman whose husband had recently met with financial difficulties.

I had a traditional marriage, the kind you hear young women today saying they'll never have. I can't say that it wasn't comfortable. I took care of the children, the house. My husband handled finances and made big decisions. We talked, but we always ended up buying the car he wanted, the house he selected. He was very sure of himself. He had more experience than I had.

We lived very well. I didn't see myself as downtrodden or weak. He was the strong male, and that was it. I wasn't out to prove I could wear the pants in the family. He was successful, and I wasn't interested in the ins and outs of his world.

The recession made an impact on our lives. He had been working on a business deal, and somewhere along the line it didn't work. The details aren't important. What is important is that he was crushed. I have never seen him like that. It was as if his world caved in. He sat brooding in the kitchen. I finally got him to talk about it. It made him feel better just telling me.

It's gotten now to the point where he'll call me during the day and talk about decisions facing him. He has never done that before. I realize that for years he has been putting on a front with me. There must have been times before this when he had business problems and never told me. I think it's easier for him now because we go through his worries together. I have always been the one dependent on him. It has brought us closer together since he's found he can talk to me —and wants to depend on me.

More important for her own personal growth is the effect of the middle-forties crisis on her sense of self. At the beginning of the crisis she may have been fearful, doubtful of her own strength. But then she learns that she can face marital difficulties, live with them, deal with them, adapt to them. This self-knowledge inevitably influences her relationship with her husband. She can respond to their differences with somewhat greater detachment. She is much less likely to react with defensive withdrawal or hostility. More positively, she comes to accept their mutual interdependency as well as their individual differences and strengths.

The End of Mothering

"I really don't want to turn back time."

There are times when the woman in her late forties daydreams about "getting away from it all," usually not to some exotic South Sea island, but to some place or some time in which she need not face the troubles of everyday life. A forty-seven-year-old woman revealed her fantasy.

Occasionally I do think of myself as free—escaping from everything. I don't think many women could ever walk out on their families, leave their homes, and children. I think men can. They do. I've known men who get a divorce, and after a few years seldom see their children. I don't know any women personally who could do this. That doesn't mean the thought hasn't entered my mind. Fantasy, though, isn't quite the same as giving up what I have now. At times I have daydreamed about myself before I was married—a young woman—and I wonder what other directions my life might have taken if I hadn't married the man I did, taken the job I did, had the children we have. It isn't often I think like this. It does happen once in a while, when I see some young woman who seems to me very much like myself at that age. The fantasy slips into my mind for a second.

By and large, these daydreams remain fantasies. They have their value in that they provide a temporary psychological escape from the tensions of reality, serving to take the edge off some trying period of life. These reveries of escape, however, are only rarely acted out, and the woman in her late forties continues to face reality.

Fortunately, by the late forties the everyday stresses of

this reality are decreasing, and life is no longer experienced as a series of problems, one after another. After the strains of adolescence, the children are entering a quieter period of young adulthood. In contrast to the feelings of tension and apprehensiveness that might have characterized a mother's emotional reactions during her children's adolescence, she is now more likely to experience a mixture of relief, joy, and pride in their growing maturity and independence—as seen in this forty-nine-year-old woman's description of her son's recent visit.

The other day our son was home for a visit, and we took a walk together. He turned to me and said he's grown up. He really feels he is an adult. The past couple of years we've watched it happen—him edging away on his own, not coming to us, not even telling us some of the things he does. I felt a twinge. Sure, he was telling me something I knew, yet hearing him say it was different from just my knowing it.

How do I feel? Sad, in a way, I suppose. Something has come to an end. It's like his room. Mostly cleared out of what belongs to him. Just a few scrapbooks and odds and ends on the shelves. Everything important in his life is emptied out of the drawers and closets. I guess I'm also sad because knowing he's grown up reminds me I'm getting older too.

While he was talking, I was surprised at what I remembered out of all the years of his childhood. I kept thinking of the day we brought him home from the hospital. It was as vivid to me as if it were yesterday. I could see his face, what he wore, me, my husband carrying him.

Anyhow, I am relieved in a way he's grown up. Living with an extra adult in the house who goes on his way while we have ours can drive you batty at times. It's nice to have it quiet at night in the house instead of music always blasting. The noise, the mess—between you and me, the laundry I don't have to do makes life a lot more pleasant. I really don't want to turn back time, even if it were possible.

It's nice seeing him working out his own life. We did. He should have the same chance. I told him I envied a lot of the things he was doing. I'm too old to do them. Hearing him tell me about all the different things he does is almost as good as doing them myself. To be honest, having him make his own day-to-day decisions lets me feel free for the first time in years— more chance to think about myself and my husband.

Life with her children is not all calm and contentment for the late-forties mother. She continues to have some worries that trouble her from time to time. But her reactions to the problems her children meet tend to shift from her previous position of intense concern. It is not that she is uninterested in, or uncaring for, her children, but in many instances she may feel that she has had enough of their problems. She would much prefer to hear about their successes, their joys and satisfactions. She may not overtly "turn off" their complaints and worries, but chances are that she pays selectively greater attention to their happier side, as seen in the comments of a mother who had recently celebrated her forty-eighth birthday.

I have to push myself to listen. I know children need to use parents as sounding boards. I get the feeling I'm at the other end of a battering ram. At times, they have me feeling I'm flat against a wall. They pound at me with this complaint and that complaint. There's no escaping. Adolescents—young adults, whatever you want to call them—can be worse than toddlers.

The other day we were sitting with our youngsters talking. They're at the point in life where everything is wrong. Nothing is right. If I try and tell them they aren't failures in my eyes, they start accusing me of lying. If I tell them they are failures, then they say I'm running them down, and why did I have them in the first place if that's the way I felt about children? You can't win with kids. I don't want to win anything. I just want a few moments' peace.

It bothers me, though, that in the outside world they're happy. They're sweet, wonderful kids. Something happens when they walk through the front door of their home. They change. I get a sullen look; one of them is pouting—life is a disaster. This seems to be a mood they've been in. I know its an age. We'll make it, though. If we made it through childhood, we can make it through adolescence. I just haven't the energy or patience to listen any more.

A friend of mine who has five children told me about how she felt about her fifth. He was coming home for spring vacation from his sophomore year in college. Her response was "I'm dreading it. I've been through it all before—the 'who am I, where am I going' monologue," as she puts it. She said at least she knows from past experience that in a little while he'll be over it— like a bad case of the flu. In the meantime she didn't want any problems, staying up until dawn having "discovering who he is" talks. I wonder if parents should tell their kids they're willing to listen to the troubles if the kids make sure to even the scoreboard with a few of the pleasures.

As she moves out of a period of strain in the family, the woman in her late forties often displays a shift in the focus of her attention. It is a shift from family problems to more positively toned activities. This may be manifested, for example, by a major restructuring of her physical surroundings, or by a marked increase of interest in home activities such as gardening or gourmet cooking, as in the case of this woman in her late forties.

For years it was a matter of feeding a hungry mob. Salad would disappear before I got the salad bowl to the table. I could barely get the knife out of a roast without hands reaching over for a piece. Now the bustle has slowed down. Kids are grown and off at school, and I can do some things I've always wanted to—like cooking. I never had the time I needed to devote to the kitchen. I love to cook, experiment with new dishes. This takes hours, and when there's a growing family around I didn't have those hours.

It's been lovely. Cooking has become quite a hobby with me. I like exotic cooking. I never could cook these dishes for my family. They'd turn up their noses and walk away from the table. My kids and my husband are a steak, French fries, and hamburger crew. Now I've even got my husband interested. We spend a lot of our weekends finding shops where we can buy foods we can't get in our local supermarket. I enjoy having dinner parties, and it's not just the food—the entire setting. I've been quite good, if I have to say so myself. In fact, several friends have asked me to hold informal cooking classes. I might just take them up on this.

These activities may represent, in part, a consolidation of her environment. Having lived through a period of emotional upheaval, she is now more concerned with establishing a stable and orderly atmosphere in which she can live and develop with a sense of psychological security.

Menopause

"Fine—it's finished."

Menopause may occur during the late forties, usually toward the end of this stage, and while it obviously involves certain physical changes, there are also important psychological issues that must be considered. The hormonal imbalance associated with menopause may result in episodes of emotional instability, rapid shifts in mood, nervousness, irritability, insomnia, and fatigue. Each of these episodes, however, is usually of fairly short duration, and after a time, the woman regains her normal equilibrium.

From the perspective of long-term personality development these temporary, physiologically determined mood shifts are not nearly as important as the psychological meaning menopause may have. In the popular literature on this topic, unfortunately the more negative reactions to menopause have been emphasized, perhaps because they elicit greater dramatic interest. Thus, fear of losing one's femininity and the depression that may be associated with this fear have been described in some detail.

Negative emotional reactions to menopause undoubtedly do occur, and when they do, the individual should of course receive professional care. However, the frequency of strong and persistent negative reactions is far less than might be suggested by the profusion of articles and books on the subject. Although the temporary mood shifts caused by hormonal imbalance at this stage are in fact a common phenomenon, the more profound, long-term fears and depressions associated with menopause do not occur among most women. In general, the woman in her late forties seems to react with equanimity to a normal, natural event.

From a psychological point of view, menopause must be considered within the overall context of each individual's pattern of psychological development. A woman's reaction to menopause, the way she interprets it, depend upon how she has responded to previous developmental crises. For example, if she has not adequately resolved the crisis of the early forties, if she is still afraid of growing old, she is quite likely to view menopause as another blow in her battle against aging. Thus, she may react with fear and anxiety, as in the case of a forty-nine-year-old woman who was beginning to experience menopausal symptoms.

> I have no great love for periods. Then again, I'm honestly scared of menopause. I've seen what's happened to friends of mine who've been through it. Their faces get wrinkled; they drag themselves around as if they are ready for the grave. It's frightening, it really is. It seems to go quickly at this point—signs of withering—and I don't want that to happen to me. I get tired of these ads that talk about growing old gracefully. There's nothing graceful about bulges and sandpaper skin. I am a firm believer in doing what you can. I know one of my friends has gone on hormones. I couldn't get over how she looked. She had reversed time. I was stunned. Her skin was lovely, and she had all the life and pep I seem to be losing. I shudder at the thought of my beginning to shrivel up.

If the woman in her late forties is still caught in the web of threats to her identity, she may well interpret menopause as yet another threat—and perhaps react with despair and depression. On the other hand, if the developmental crisis of the early forties has been resolved, and the shakiness of identity experienced during the middle forties is in the process of resolution, a woman is most likely to react to menopause with some temporary discomfort and shifts in mood, but without undue emotional strain. In this instance, menopause is viewed as just another step in a lifelong process of physical development, a step that marks the end of one physiological era and the beginning of another that involves freedom from some degree of discomfort and concern. A forty-nine-year-old woman beginning menopause reflected this more positive point of view.

You won't find me crying the day I stop getting the "curse." I wonder sometimes about all this talk—mostly by men it seems—about how women are up-tight about menopause. I could do without the scares, and there *have* been scares of waiting for a late period and wondering if I'm pregnant.

I can remember years ago when I was in high school —long before it was easy for a woman to get an abor-tion—one of my friends' mothers was going to have a baby. Gossip went around like wildfire. The girl was ashamed to come to school. It was awful for the family. Everyone kept saying the woman's forty-nine—people talked as if she had committed a crime. There was an older boy in the family, and he wouldn't talk to his mother. He was that embarrassed. We forget what it was like years ago. Thank goodness women have more of a right to make decisions about their own bodies in this day and age.

Back to myself. I've had my moments of fear. Once I even went for a test. I was in a panic because I was two weeks late. It's not only worry about a baby. Seven days are gone out of every month of my life. I flow pretty heavily. The first day or two of every period, there are times I can't leave the house. I accept all the discomfort. That's a price I pay for being a woman. Don't tell me, though, that the end of that era won't be welcomed. I'll say to myself, I went through it; fine —it's finished. I won't have one single regret.

The sense of freedom sometimes experienced after menopause may be accompanied by heightened sexual drive and interest, as reflected in the following remarks.

I always wondered what it will be like just to have sex without getting ready, thinking about the calendar, safe periods, contraceptives. Even then there's a nagging worry there's been a slip. Goodness knows, everyone hears enough horror stories about slips during the change of life to make one concerned. Now that I'm through with periods, I don't wonder any more. Let me tell you, it's great. Men certainly have the edge. They haven't had a lifetime of worries. I feel like I should start making up for lost time. It's not a bad idea, now that I think about it.

Outside the Home

"It's important to be involved helping others in a personal sort of way."

As the tensions in the family are reduced, the woman in her late forties may devote more of her energy to interests outside the home. Although this shift is in some respects similar to the pattern of behavior shown in the early forties, both the nature and meaning of these activities are likely to be different at this stage.

During her early forties, in addition to whatever intrinsic value various community activities might have had, the opportunity for social interaction with her peers was a major source of satisfaction and reward. For example, while she might have been sincerely interested in working toward improvement of her community's schools, she also derived satisfaction from the opportunity to work with others in achieving this goal.

For the late-forties woman, the motivation is likely to be quite different. She, too, is interested in relationships with others outside of the family, and undoubtedly derives satisfaction from them. However, the chief value is usually tied more closely to the activity itself—the social welfare, political or educational goals toward which she contributes. A forty-eight-year-old woman discussed the satisfactions she derived from being involved in a program for visiting the homebound.

An organization I used to be active with called me and asked if I would serve on a theater benefit committee. I said no, a flat no. That kind of service doesn't appeal to me. I've been through it—lunches, fashion shows, donor parties. I can't say they weren't enjoyable at the time. Now that kind of life seems empty and pointless. It isn't that we didn't do some good. I won't say that. It's simply a fact that at my age, time is precious. I can't see wasting energy on another luncheon or sitting with the telephone calling lists of names.

What I do now is different. A friend of mine persuaded me to join a group that spend a few hours a week visiting homebound. We visit all sorts of people —children, aged, blind—anyone who can't get out and needs outside stimulation. They're not necessarily poor. Some of them are. Handing out money isn't our purpose. I got out once a week for a morning and read books and newspapers to an elderly blind man who can't get around. He has a heart condition. It's not at all depressing. He's better able to accept life than I have been sometimes.

What I do isn't much—read baseball scores, baseball reports. Sometimes we just talk, or I'll run an errand. A homemaker comes in every afternoon to do housework. I fill another gap. I'm a friend. I know I leave his little apartment with a very different kind of feeling than I had getting dressed for a luncheon. My friends who volunteer at hospitals feel the same way. All of us believe it's important to be involved helping others in a personal sort of way.

Old Friends

"No act, no pretense, no going through barriers."

During the stressful periods of the middle forties, friends may provide a valuable source of reassurance and support. Friends continue to be important to the woman in her late forties; however, the pattern of social interaction tends to become somewhat more focused and delimited. Specifically, she is usually less interested in expanding her circle of acquaintance, and more likely to place greater value on maintaining relationships with a few old friends, people with whom she feels comfortable and secure. Rather than go out of her way to meet new people, social life usually involves people she has known for some time, as in the case of a woman in her late forties who talked about the importance of old friends.

Old friends are special. Years ago we liked meeting lots of new people. Now it's different. We don't seem to have the same interest or energy. We've reached an age where we like to spend time with a few good friends. We recently realized how we've changed. An old friend, someone we've known for years called. We hadn't seen him for months. We didn't even have that much to talk about. Our lives have gone separate ways. It didn't matter. He's a good friend, and we don't always need topics to relate to him. Just the pleasantness of keeping in touch over the years is enough. There isn't any ceremony. We didn't have to go through the "Who are you?" "Where did you go to school?" "What kind of work are you in?" routines. You know how it is at cocktail parties or evenings where you sit with a whole group of people you're meeting for the first time.

We were at a party recently, and suddenly I had this feeling of being out of it. The people were nice, but we knew we wouldn't ever see any of them again. It was a "Hi, there," "Hello, there" evening. Pleasant but not satisfying. I can feel the difference when an old close friend calls on the telephone. The voice alone is familiar—no act, no pretense, no going through "getting to know each other" barriers. These kinds of relationships take time to build. Maybe at our age you know you don't have all the time in the world to start up with new friendships.

Fulfillment

"I was happy."

The scramble and striving for status and position that might have characterized previous years at work are much less evident in the late forties. By this stage, a woman has probably achieved a position of considerable responsibility, perhaps not with the degree of public recognition she might once have needed and wanted, but a position in which she can use her talents and experience. The work itself becomes more important, and she is often concerned with doing something she feels is intrinsically worthwhile rather than pursuing status and promotion as ends in themselves.

Interestingly enough, it is occasionally at this time that a woman's career may be significantly advanced, not so much because she in fact deserved it, but because circumstances at work may have made it impossible to avoid promoting her. This is not a highly common occurrence, but when a woman in her late forties does receive the status she may have hoped for, she often seems to react with a kind of wry humor and a certain perspective on herself that she might have been incapable of a few years earlier. A woman of forty-eight who had just received a major promotion commented on her reactions.

Everyone at the office asked me what I did to celebrate. I got the promotion I should have gotten ten years before. I don't dare tell them what I really did. On my way home I stopped at the cleaners and went through a lot of unidentified sweaters looking for a favorite blue one of mine they had lost. I found it. The manager was happy; I was happy. He said to me, "It's your lucky day." The sweater had been missing for a month.

I stopped off at the grocery. I was angry at myself

when I bought that beast of a cat of mine chicken livers as a treat. She goes insane about chicken livers. In fact, when I walked into the apartment she nearly clawed me and the bag. Pure joy on that cat's miserable face. I'm always threatening to get rid of her. Then I did the laundry, which had been piling up for days. That's the evening of celebration I spent.

Of course, I am pleased. I like the salary increase, the title, the new office. To say that I'm going to do a dance of joy or make a big thing of it would be false. It's come at the wrong time in my life for an all-out celebration. Ten years ago it would have been different. I guess I worked so long without expecting a major promotion that it still isn't registering. I suppose I'll have a few close friends in for dinner this weekend. I'd have them over anyway.

In the process of restructuring her own identity, the late-forties woman moves beyond the bounds of interpersonal relationships that have heretofore probably been the major concerns of her life. To be sure, family, intimate friends, and perhaps one or two colleagues at work continue to be profoundly important. However, another dimension of psychological functioning assumes increasing significance. It is a growing concern about the meaningfulness of her life. This concern is illustrated by a forty-nine-year-old woman's comments about her renewal of interest in religion.

Religion has a very different meaning for me at my age than it did when I was young. As a child, I went to church because I was sent, not because I wanted to go. There was another period in life when I was active in clubs. I did my share in running bazaars, dinners. People still talk about one festival we had with a cabaret and dancing in the church basement. None of these things had much to do with religion, except raising funds. All these things are less important now. The religious part of church life is beginning to mean more to me than I'm ready to admit. I find myself thinking about the church's teachings.

I'm not trying to present myself as a philosopher—far from it. I do think about the teachings, the rituals and what they mean in my life. I think about what comes after life. After you have lived a while, had experiences, had joys and heartaches of life, at age fifty you do start to think about moral and spiritual values. It's a time in life when going to church is more than sitting through services.

The concern about the meaningfulness of life is not limited to religious interests. For some, religion plays little or no part in this particular aspect of late-forties development. The search for meaning may take many different forms; it may involve political, ethical, social, intellectual, aesthetic values; but the central core is a woman's need to reintegrate her identity on a basis that extends beyond immediate interpersonal relationships.

In most instances, this issue is not resolved before the end of the decade of the forties. It may remain a problem that will occupy a woman for the rest of her life. Nevertheless, the concern to find ultimate fulfillment, even though unverbalized, and for many not even consciously recognized as such, adds a certain depth to her life and to her personality.

We cannot end our discussion of the woman in her late forties with a simple, neat resolution of the developmental tasks she faces. Life usually doesn't happen that way. Instead, we must leave her at a point of dynamic change. She has lived through the crisis of her early forties, faced the signs of aging, adapted and matured as a result. She has met the crisis of her middle forties, dealt with the seemingly endless problems of everyday living, withstood the threats to her identity, and maintained her psychological integration and integrity. Now, in her late forties, she is resolving yet another crisis; she is facing the challenge of redefining herself and restructuring her life, of changing, adapting, growing. As she enters the decade of her fifties, she is in the process of fulfilling her own individual potential as a unique and valuable person.

conclusion

Several years ago we needed a new car. Our sensible, black, four-door with rear and front seats and an ample trunk for groceries, tools, and bags of leaves at fall cleaning time was giving in to age. Our children were almost adults. They weren't going to sit in the back seats and stuff gum wrappers into ash trays; they weren't going to litter the floor with mix-and-match socks, gloves, and sneakers.

At forty-five when one considers the purchase of a new car, the thought of style enters into choices. The automobile salesman, an energetic thirty-year-old man, wasn't quite on our wavelength. He kept pushing us toward cars with four doors, comfortable rear and front seats, and spacious trunks. When we showed a preference for a white convertible with two red leather bucket seats, a body that threatened to scrape the pavements, and a trunk that with some juggling could hold a partially filled shopping bag, our salesman seemed to react negatively.

"Anything wrong?" we asked.

"No, it's your choice," he told us.

"Not yours?" we inquired.

"Sure, it's my idea of a car, but you people—I mean you're . . ." he faltered.

"Too old?"

"No, not at all. It's just that *kids* like this kind of car. You know what I mean?"

When we brought the car home, our oldest son was confused.

"Whose car is that?"

"Your parents'."

"You bought that car?"

"Anything wrong?"

"You're kidding." It was our car. What had he thought? Later on we learned that he had had a flicker of wishful thinking when he saw the car. He thought we had bought him a graduation present.

No one, least of all the automobile industry, has ruled that after-forties can't buy a little convertible with a canvas top. But in our culture, mature adults apparently belong in "mature" cars, which means practical cars with four doors, big seats, and the unwritten word, "conventional," stamped on the front hood.

Our shift from a four-door sedan to a little white convertible represented only one of the changes we went through during our forties. There were other, probably more important, changes that we experienced ourselves and observed among the people we talked to in the course of preparing this book. In fact, by far the most important discovery we made in our own lives, as well as in the process of studying others living through their forties, was the fact that this time of life can be an exciting and dynamic period of psychological growth and development.

The period of life after forty often involves a good deal of personal stress. There are frustrations, anxieties, and responsibilities which none of us can escape. This certainly doesn't mean that every single person experiences the identical set of personal upheavals. Each of us is an individual and not a carbon copy of someone else. What we do mean is that after forty, and forty isn't a magic number but rather an approximate midpoint in life, there is frequently considerable unrest, dissatisfaction, and psychological turbulence. But it is precisely this turbulence that serves as a motivation for very significant psychological growth.

Life after forty, perhaps more than any other time in

adulthood, provides opportunities for enormous psychological gains. In our culture we expect children and young adults to grow and change psychologically. We also expect adults past forty to be stabilized. There is discomfort, humor, and dismay when adults in their forties and beyond discard established routines, shift their lifestyles, or alter their behaviors. When young children and adults change, we are pleased and call the changes healthy growth. When older adults change, it is regarded with suspicion. Nevertheless, change after forty is often a sign of healthy, positive growth.

We are in no way suggesting that people after forty should toss aside their lifestyles and experiment with entirely new ways of living. We are not implying that it is always healthy or good to arbitrarily restructure our lives after forty, discard old responsibilities, or search for new adventures. But we *should* recognize and appreciate that this is a time of life that offers tremendous opportunities for growth and development. Yes, it is often a time of stress, tension, and troubles, but even more important in the long run, it is a time when we can more fully realize our own unique potentials as mature adults.

Recognizing the opportunities of the past forty years is an important first step in the process of growth, and the process itself is enhanced by understanding yourself. This doesn't mean that understanding yourself automatically leads to psychological growth. But self-awareness and insight into what you are experiencing can take the edge off feelings of tension, anxiety, moodiness, and anger. Rather than suffer the doubts of what is happening to yourself in the post-forty years, knowledge and understanding can help you cope actively with the stresses you encounter. Through self-understanding you gain greater tolerance for yourself and also gain greater confidence in your own potential for growth.

As John Milton said many years ago, "To know that which before us lies in daily life is prime wisdom." Knowing what to expect, knowing what stresses and frustrations are not only typical but normal, is a first step in preparing yourself for your own growth. And that is the primary purpose of this book—to provide you with a basis for gaining greater understanding of yourself. By sharing with you our own observations and the experiences of others, we hope that you can gain some perspective on your own experiences. Through understanding others who have lived through this period of life, you can learn to understand yourself more fully, and thus achieve even greater self-realization.

appendix:

Twenty Exercises in Personal Growth

Here is a program designed to help you use this book to understand yourself and those with whom you live. It is a program designed to help you use this book not just as interesting reading, but as a dynamic tool to help you grow, not just survive, in the years after your fortieth birthday.

May we suggest some basic guidelines that will help to make this program work for you and those with whom you share it. They apply whether you work the exercises alone, with the someone closest to you, or with a group.

- *Identify—don't compare.* Don't get caught up in the age, sex, or personal history of the persons in the book. Use their stories to help you identify questions and especially feelings in your own life.
- *Listen.* Before you talk . . . listen. Let the people in the book speak, let others speak, let your inner self speak . . . and listen to them all before you start talking.
- *Take it easy.* One exercise at a time is enough. It may even be too much.
- *Make the book and program work for you.* Don't get caught on our outline. Arrange your discussions in the way that works best for you. And, above all, don't get stuck with using just our questions. When you listen to yourself and others, you may hear better questions than these.

- *Plan.* But don't overdo it. If you are working in a large
group, you'll need an announced time and place and
somebody to organize groupings. But don't get too much
more complicated than this. All you really need is the
book, the right people, and the honesty of your own feelings.
- *Keep it simple.* Each of the exercises has a simple outline.
  —We suggest readings (specific chapters in the book that
  you will find helpful). Read them in advance or when you
  get together. Both he and she should read both *Him* and
  Her and *We.*
  —As a stimulus for the session, we have phrased an idea
  to use as a springboard into the mood and direction of the
  suggested questions.
  —Questions for reflection are what they say they are. Use
  these questions or your own to provide the points of your
  exercise.
  —"Coming down" is our word for looking back on the
  exercise. Some of you may want to remain where you met.
  Others might want to meet at a pre-arranged place for
  coffee, tea, and so on. You may prefer a journal. For
  couples, home is probably not the best place. But do talk
  it over, preferably within twenty-four hours.
- *Do read the book.* You will be your own best resource. But
  the experience of others can enrich your own reflection.
  And if you are working in large groups, you may want to
  have the book available for sale.

Session 1: The Pace of Life

*The simple statement "first things first" somehow
can make us stop even the most hectic pace to
figure out just what are the* first things.

Suggested reading:
HIM: pages 21–23
HER: pages 131–134

For reflection:
1. Do you find yourself feeling lost in a treadmill of activities?
2. Are you running from one thing to another to catch up with yourself?
3. Have you recently stopped and asked yourself: "Is what I am now doing what I really want to do? While I am doing this, what am I thinking about? What would I rather be doing?"
4. Try applying the questions in number three to an experience in the last twenty-four hours of your life.
5. What would you have eliminated from your activities of the last twenty-four hours that could have made you feel more comfortable with yourself?

Coming down:
Make a list of things you resent doing. Suggest some that could be dropped. Try to figure out how you can make some of those tasks and situations more comfortable for you, even if you cannot eliminate them entirely.

Session 2:   Fat and Forty

Perhaps a simple way to handle a negative trait or self-destructive behavior is to say either "I'm really too nice to punish myself that way" or "I deserve better."

Suggested reading:
HIM: pages 25–29
HER: pages 134–143

For reflection:

1. Do you find yourself using your age or aging as an excuse for your physical appearance?
2. Do you rationalize and say that there is nothing you can do about increased weight because you're getting older?
3. List some reasons why you believe your age group is more inclined to be "out of shape." In what ways is it OK to be "out of shape" because of "your age"?
4. Instead of not eating food that puts on extra pounds, do you spend time simply talking about losing weight? Have you ever sought help in controlling your weight and general physical appearance? Who can help you not eat the foods that harm you? Do your family or friends help or hinder you in your appearance?

Coming down:
Choose one food item that you feel helps damage your appearance. Think about the phrase "I deserve better." Try giving yourself a twenty-four-hour gift of doing without just one food or habit that takes away from your appearance. If it works, why not try it for just another twenty-four hours.

Session 3: The Signs of Ripening

This is the time to take a good look at yourself: body, mind, and spirit. Try not to judge what you see, hear, and feel. As you look at the "signs of ripening," try to discover new areas of comfort and strength you have found, developed, or maintained.

Suggested reading:
HIM: pages 25–29
HER: pages 143–145

For reflection:
1. Are you aware of any physical changes in yourself that seem to be troublesome? Poor eyesight, poor hearing, fatigue?
2. What has been your reaction to these changes?
3. Have you shared your concerns with someone? Rather than blaming age or planning to do something about these things on another day, have you done something about them?
4. Have you recognized that taking care of oneself physically, like any other of life's responsibilities, should be a part of your life?

Coming down:
List some ways in which you could be good to yourself today. Try doing one of these things *just for you* in the next twenty-four hours.

Session 4:   The Rumblings of Crises

"Easy does it, but do it." There is, however, a difference between stagnation and going easy. What we do with comfort, that's what we "easy do." Problems, sameness, and confusions often lead us to stagnation, but they can lead us to growth and sharing.

Suggested reading:
HIM: pages 25–29
HER: pages 168–170

For reflection:
1. Are you worried about how things are going in your work (job or otherwise)? Do you use your age as an excuse for

not moving ahead or for lack of success or enthusiasm?

2. Do you find yourself getting bothered about small problems (thorns in your side) that didn't bother you before?

3. Are you feeling bored, frustrated, or dissatisfied with your work? Have you thought of changing jobs or roles within your home? Do you feel you have advanced and been appreciated in your work as rapidly, or as much, as you had hoped for?

4. Have you tried sharing your feelings to numbers 1–3 above with anyone close to you—family, friends, lover, husband, wife?

Coming down:

Try picking out one "thorn" in your daily existence that really bothers you. Share it with one other person. Don't ask them for a solution or answer. Ask them to tell you what they understood your problem to be and how you felt about it. Whatever follows in the sharing is a bonus.

Session 5: The Question of Identity

Supporting one another rather than having an attitude of criticism and judgment is most difficult when we are uncertain and in turmoil. Sometimes it's better to stop and look at yourself and find just one thing about you that makes you satisfied. Keep it something simple and enjoy that aspect of yourself for a while.

Suggested reading:
WE: pages 14–16
HER: pages 158–161

For reflection:

1. Do you find yourself focusing on *you* to the point that you are losing awareness of what's happening in the important relationships in your life?
2. How much time would you guess that you spend concentrating on your successes, failures, interests, activities, and dislikes? Do others around you seem to be "hurt" by you more often than in the past?
3. Taking stock of where you are psychologically is extremely important. Are you also, however, remembering to take stock of what's going on in the lives of those who are close to you?

Coming down:
Think of something you would like done for you. Try doing it for someone else. Try picking something that you can do for someone in a way that they wouldn't know who did it for them.

Session 6: The Discomfited Past

"Yesterday is gone and all you have is today!"
When we accept responsibility for our acts
and decisions, we always have the option
to change—even if we only change our attitude
toward the act or decision. All we can change,
after all, is us.

Suggested reading:
WE: pages 16–18
HER: pages 230–233

For reflection:

1. Do you find yourself regularly looking backward instead of forward?
2. Do you eagerly, or even unendingly, keep reminding those closest to you about the successes of your past? Do you find that at times you exaggerate the importance of these successes?
3. Do you bemoan and recount your failures, missed opportunities, and defeats? How important, really, are they today?

Coming down:

Just for today, look for things to enjoy. Tell those around you about those things you notice that go well for you today. Again, keep it simple. Something as small as not having the toast burn can begin a great day. Keep looking for things. Make a list and share it.

Session 7:   Intimations of Mortality

Illness and death are limitations, but perhaps even more limiting than either is fear.
Fear somehow touches every aspect of our lives.
For all our efforts, few of us can attain freedom from fear. In each day we can muster the courage to deal constructively with whatever fears remain.

Suggested reading:
WE: pages 7–9
HER: pages 145–146

For reflection:

1. Have you found yourself thinking about illness and death more frequently than you used to?

2. Have you or any of your friends or relatives been seriously ill recently? Has anyone you've known, perhaps someone close to your own age, died in the past year or so?
3. What are your own feelings about being ill? How do you usually deal with being ill? What role do doctors, medications, hospitals, your church, family, and closest loved ones play in the way you deal with sickness?
4. What are your own feelings about death? How have you faced your own mortality and the fact that you, too, must die? What role do doctors, medications, hospitals, your church, family, and closest loved ones play in your thoughts about death? Have you talked to anyone about your feelings?

Coming down:
For all the things we seem to be able to control and manage in our lives, illness and death seem to be totally unmanageable. Take time to think of some other things that are unmanageable by you (the sun rising, the rain on a day you've planned a picnic, an unexpected visit by a dear friend). Make a list of a few of these things. Accept them as facts. Illness and death . . . what are they?

Session 8: The Threat of Impotence

Demands we place upon ourselves inevitably translate into demands upon others. The more we feel "small" within ourselves, the more we look to others to give us the meaning and power to act. To be humanly sexual we have to find both the humanity and power to act within ourselves. When we seek either outside ourselves we invite domination, rejection—we feel neither human nor sexual—and powerlessness.

Suggested reading:
HIM: pages 34–37
HER: pages 145–149

For reflection:
1. Do you find yourself "slowing up" sexually? Have you been at all worried or concerned about your own sexuality?
2. Do worry, fatigue, or anxiety interfere with your sex life? How do these things make you feel about sex and your sexual relationships?
3. When you have had worries or concerns about your sexuality and sexual relationships, how have you reacted? Have you chosen to blame your partner? Have you blamed yourself? What have you done to deal with the situation? Have you shared your concerns with anyone? To what effect?

Coming down:
Many of the frustrations and confusions of our lives are due to our failure to deal with tasks and problems in order of importance. Sometimes just getting things in order, or putting "first things first," eases enough tension and frustration that we can be more at ease with ourselves. Choose something that bothers you to act on today. Choose something small. Make sure it's something you can accomplish today. When you've finished, tell yourself what a good job you've done. Then try telling someone else without letting your enjoyment of this completed task depend on their reaction. Share the joy of the task done. Wallow in it. You deserve it.

Session 9:   The Family Rut

Family is a place where we can share our identity.
Family can be a place of sharing experience,
strength, and hope. No family, no matter how
supportive or how much in need of us,
can be our identity.

Suggested reading:
HIM: pages 37–44 and 65–72
HER: pages 158–161 and 194–199

For reflection:
1. Do you feel that your family life has fallen into a rut? How does that make you feel about yourself?
2. Do you feel overburdened by petty responsibilities?
3. Are you dissatisfied with your children? Do you feel they are spoiled and unappreciative? What choices do they make that conflict with your values, opinions, and feelings? What do you do about it?
4. Have you talked to your partner or children about your feelings?

Coming down:
When we try to make situations work the way we think they *should,* we are often disappointed, if not totally frustrated. Manipulating others just doesn't bring us comfort even when it appears that we have "our way." Manipulation of spouse, child, or parent leads to resistance on their part. Then we develop hurt feelings, a sense of persecution, and a desire to retaliate. Try watching your family today. See what they do without being told. Listen to what they say when you don't correct them. (You may have to try this several times over a period of days if you have a track record for "running the show.") Your family may give you a lot. By

taking a day off from "running the show" you may have found time to be comfortable with yourself.

Session 10:   Explosions

Self-righteous anger can be very enjoyable. It enables us to store up, until the "appropriate" moment, all our disappointments with our own failings, defects, and self-questioning. In a very perverse way we can take delight in the annoyance or injustice of others. From our own discomfort with ourselves comes a feeling of superiority.

Suggested reading:
HIM: pages 47–52
HER: pages 210–212

For reflection:
1. Have you felt moody lately? Have you been "down in the dumps"? Do you feel there are more things wrong than right with your world?
2. Do you find yourself losing your temper more readily than you used to?
3. Do you find yourself getting tense and anxious without any apparent reason?

Coming down:
When disturbed, your first thought may be to quiet the disturbance. Sometimes, however, we choose to dwell on and wallow in our misery. Next time you get angry or annoyed about something, or about someone's behavior, *stop.* Try making a list. Don't limit your list to what is bothering you now. List all the people, institutions, policies, laws with

which you are angry. Put the list away for at least twenty-four hours to gain some distance. After this time has passed, write a letter explaining why each of the items on your list bothers you. Try being as honest as you can. Which items threaten your pride? Which make you question your self-esteem? Which are brought about because you feel your ambitions have been frustrated? Which are brought about because your personal relationships, goals, and plans did not go the way you planned? Put the letter away. Forget it, or put it in the wastebasket. That's how things *were*. *Now* you can get on with living today.

Session 11: The Rut

There are times when we feel out of phase. There are moments of pain and separation as we go about our business of growth. Growth comes from choosing. The most important choice is today.

Suggested reading:
HIM: pages 88–94
HER: pages 152–157 and 163–165

For reflection:
1. Have you recently felt that you should cut loose from what you've been doing, break out of the rut, or change the way you've been living?
2. If you have felt this way, have you thought about the reasons for your feelings? Have you done anything about these feelings?
3. What benefit would change bring to your life today? How much change would be required for you to be comfortable? How will you handle the pain and confusion of change?

Coming down:
Change is surely no way to avoid pain, and it gives no guarantee of comfort. We can only live one day at a time. As you begin your day, remember you do not have to face your whole life—just today. There is a spiritual axiom that says every time we are disturbed, no matter what the cause, something is wrong with us. When frustrated, feeling "frozen in place," confused about major issues and conflicts within and without, *stop*. Remember you can choose to stay . . . to go . . . but, more importantly, you can choose to be you *today*.

Session 12:   The Conjugal Battleground

In special relationships like marriage, we too often seek all meaning, all activity, and all purpose of life. Genuine long-term efforts are made at keeping things together—providing the right kind of home for the children or doing things that "should" make us happy. When this "father-knows-best" effort seems doomed to failure, we find our whole identity, all meaning, all of our living threatened. Often we react without taking a close look. Unconsidered decisions never lead to comfort.

Suggested reading:
HIM: pages 52–65
HER: pages 145–149

For reflection:
1. Have you been arguing or fighting with your spouse

more often than you used to? If not, do the arguments seem to have a greater disruptive force in your life?

2. If you have been fighting, has it been with your partner or within yourself? What have the fights been about? What have you been angry about?

3. How do the fights usually get started? What happens? How do they get resolved? Have you been especially hurt?

4. Do you feel your spouse doesn't understand you? What is the basis for this feeling?

5. Are you bored or dissatisfied with your relationship? Have you talked to your spouse about your feelings? How does your spouse feel? If you haven't talked with your spouse, have you shared your feelings with anyone else? Have you looked for companionship outside your marriage? How do you feel today?

Coming down:
Expectations which build in our minds often get in the way of the good life we can enjoy. "Father knows best" may have been a great model for a television show, but as a way of day-to-day living it just doesn't work. What would you like to obtain *today* from sharing your life with another person? Try to forget, for a while, how and why you are in your current situation. Just list the qualities of a relationship that would make you feel comfortable, if not always happy. Note especially the kind of partner you would like to share your life with. List the qualities of such a relationship and partner. *Stop.* See how many of those qualities you possess *today.* Be thankful for those you already have. Choose one you do not have, and try to act as if you were that kind of person. How does it feel? Try sharing this exercise with your spouse or the person in your special relationship.

Session 13:   The Game of Work

*Work not only occupies a large percentage of our
time, but it also speaks to and is part of our
preoccupations. No one really works for money.
Part of the picture can indeed be economic
survival, but there is more. The attitudes we have
about ourselves influence what we do and how we
feel about it. What we do and how we feel about
it affect, and are part of, the total picture of who
we see ourselves as being. Thus, even the thought
of changing from an unhappy work situation can
be paralyzing.*

Suggested reading:
HIM: pages 82–87
HER: pages 149–152 and 199–206

For reflection:
1. Have you thought about changing jobs, doing something else? If so, what are the reasons for the change?
2. Have you done anything about changing? How do you feel about the chances of changing? Have you talked to others about your desire to change?
3. If you were to change jobs (or get a job), what would you be looking for other than money?
4. What are the realistic possibilities for change? How do you think the change would affect you? Your family? The persons with whom you now work?

Coming down:
Our business is to make the kinds of life choices that bring us beyond survival. Most of us, even in the worst situations, can survive. The comfort gained from choosing behavior which is consistent with our values, attitudes, and feelings

cannot help but bring serenity. It is within that context that we deal with change, questions, and, ultimately, growth.

Session 14: The Seriousness of Games

Being playful, whether it means how we approach life or a tennis game, can be a source of great comfort. Playfulness is that willingness to be open to new and different experiences. Games provide a license to try without having to be the best or the most successful. Sure, we can turn even games into work, but openness enables us to be pleased with ourselves for just trying.

Suggested reading:
HIM: pages 88–92
HER: pages 158–163

For reflection:
1. Have you found yourself becoming more interested in some physical activity recently, such as jogging, golf, tennis, or any other sport?
2. Are you concerned about getting "out of shape"? If so, what have you done, or what are you doing, about it? Why?
3. Have you become interested in a wider range of activities than you used to be? Have you been doing things, reading things, seeing things that you didn't pay much attention to a few years ago?

Coming down:
Make a list of things that you did as a child that you stopped doing when you grew up. Think about those childhood

activities which would give you pleasure or just plain enjoyment *today*. Include one of those activities in your schedule next week. You might even want to share it with someone.

Session 15: Shifting Values

Usually, when we value someone or something, we choose to act in ways which tell us and those around us what is important to us. But sometimes when we, with or without the help of others, look at our day-to-day behavior, we find ourselves acting in ways which seem contrary to what we've claimed to be valuable. Sometimes we adjust our behavior to reflect our values. Other times we take time to examine what we claim to be our values and see if they "mesh" with where we are and want to be today.

Suggested reading:
HIM: pages 111–123
HER: pages 163–165 and 182–191

For reflection:
1. Have you spent some time thinking about your basic values, about who and what is important to you? About what you've done in life? About your future goals?
2. How would you like to develop and grow over the next years? Would you have to change in what and whom you value in order to do so? How do you feel about such changes, growth, and development *today?*

Coming down:
Before we can redirect ourselves or grow, we have to reflect

on what is and take time to adjust to that. Our greatest stumbling block may be the desire to totally change everything to suit ourselves today. Instead of doing something to change yourself, *today* try to like who you are and what you have. For today, save yourself from worry, hurry, and indecision by relaxing just long enough to realize what *life is.*

Session 16:   Putting It Back Together

Often in life we ask for space to handle people and situations. There are times when we try to rearrange furniture, daily schedules, and even other people's lives to achieve the space we need. Even when we are willing to give others space to live and let live, we find it difficult to give ourselves the space we need to be comfortable with whom we are.

Suggested reading:
HIM: pages 101–110 and 123–128
HER: pages 167–170

For reflection:
1. In what ways have you changed and developed over the past five or six years? Do you have a wider range of interests than you had before?
2. Do you feel you are more inner-directed, less influenced by the opinions of others? Are you more confident of yourself and do you find yourself needing less approval from others? Are you less concerned about the external signs of success?
4. Are you aware of other people's feelings? In your relationship with your partner, do you find yourself able to be more appreciative of your interdependence?

5. Are you more tolerant of other people, more accepting of differences among people? Do you feel that you appreciate yourself—your talents, abilities, and special qualities? Do you find you have a greater appreciation for the experience, strength, and hope that others possess? Do you have a greater, clearer sense of who you are, where you've been in life, and where you're going?

Coming down:
Each of us is entitled to a personal view of things, but we have no right to inflict that view on anyone else. Look at yourself. Think about all the things you like about yourself. Think about the people who really like you. Think about those who love you. How have they come to know and to love you?

Session 17:   Growing Apart

In relationships, people sometimes feel that they are growing apart. Often what is happening is that one or both of the partners fears "falling apart." Personal stress situations from inside and outside always show up in the relationship. Losing interest in yourself is a definite way to lose interest in another person—even a special one. Just as destructive to a relationship is losing room for one another.

Suggested reading:
WE: pages 11–13
HIM: pages 111–123
HER: pages 170–182

For reflection:

1. Are you watching for signs that show you may be drifting apart from your partner?
2. Are you so busy worrying about your own identity that you are forgetting to be interested and concerned with the identities of people closest to you?
3. Are you concerned about breaking loose from your "comfortable" rut, your familiar world, and blaming your partner for holding you back?
4. Are you making an effort to involve your partner in your new interests and activities?
5. Are you relying on age as the reason why you are closing down and narrowing your horizons to the paths of your first forty years?

Coming down:

Sometimes, even after many years of living with ourselves, we are surprised to learn something about ourselves that we just never knew. Try to think about a recent experience in which you discovered something you like about yourself but were previously unaware of. Now think of a similar situation in which you learned something you like about your partner that you were previously unaware of. If you have not yet done so, take time soon to share your discoveries with your partner.

Session 18:   The Affair

*If we lean too heavily on people, they will sooner
or later fail us, for they are human and cannot
possibly meet our incessant needs and demands.
Somehow when we feel most "at a loss" we
actually feel that we are "lost." One temporary
way to gain control is to create or to find ourselves
in a temporary situation. Call it an affair, or call it
anything you want. It enables us to control at least
a part of our lives. It fulfills at least some of the
need. It means that we don't have to admit that
we are "lost," that we "need."*

Suggested reading:
HIM: pages 72–81
HER: pages 161–163

For reflection:
1. Instead of waiting and wondering what's happening to
   your sexual relationship with your partner, have you
   made an effort to discuss the problem? Your needs? Your
   desires? Your fears?
2. Are you assigning blame? Have you been digging your
   heels in, thinking, "Let her/him make the first advances.
   I'm always the one to do the approaching"?
3. Have you tried to kid yourself into thinking that everything is perfect within you and your way of dealing with
   the relationship when you have been aware that sexual
   relations between the two of you have stopped or have
   been strained?

Coming down:
Our sexual behavior tells us a lot about how we feel about

ourselves. Wholesome sexuality demands two persons who are willing to share more than just organs. Think about the ways in which your sexual life with your partner gives/gave you joy. Think about a time when you felt your partner really enjoyed you sexually. How did you know? How did it make you feel? Did you ever discuss these times with your partner? A touch and a word of honesty can be one of the greatest sexual experiences, eliminating mounds of jealousy, distrust, and crippling possessiveness. What would you like to communicate to your partner through your next sexual experience?

Session 19:   The Children Leave

Someone has said that the perfect parent's prayer is: "Thy will, not mine, be done." Family is where we can be "with" each other. Even the smallest child can have a unique identity and have a place "with" everyone else. So often in our desire as parents and children we try to be and to do the best. Too often, we spend our energies trying to protect and to do what is best for others, wasting the energy that could be turned into the love and concern we share "with" each other. There are no perfect parents. There are no perfect children. When parents spend their lives trying to create either the perfect world for their children or the perfect children, not only do they fail, but when the children are gone, so is their reason for living.

Suggested reading:
HIM: pages 37–44 and 65–72
HER: pages 191–199

For reflection:

1. Have you left your children's rooms exactly as they were long after the children have left home? In what subtle ways are you still behaving as if the children were still living at home?
2. Are you helping yourself recover from the empty-nest blues through outside activities or new interests? Have you let your children go? How often do you call them? How often do you expect them to see or to call you?
3. Are you willing to let yourself grow up and change as you grow older? Do you still ask yourself "what will the children think?" before taking an action in your own life? What effect does this have on your decision making?
4. Are you able to recognize that growing up and changing doesn't have to mean throwing over everything you are or have been—yet that there is more?

Coming down:
Take a look at your family life. What are some of the best things you've done *with* your children? What are some of the best things you've done *with* your partner? How do you feel about those things today? Have you ever told your children or partner how you feel? What are some of the things you did *for* your children? What are some of the things you did *for* your partner? How do you feel about those things today? Which things give you more joy today—what you've done *for* or *with* your family?

Session 20: Menopause

The closer one approaches menopause, the easier it is to reach a decision that your procreative responsibility is fulfilled. Menopause is "no pause" from being a responsible, loving, human person. Menopause is a call for both partners to continue to be co-creators. Physiologically, psychologically, and spiritually, this experience, like most times of growth, involves pain and even a kind of death. Two loving persons can share the fears, pains, and anxieties of this time. Two loving persons can be freed to give love to each other.

Suggested reading:
HIM: pages 123–128
HER: pages 223–226

For reflection:
1. Are you convincing yourself that menopause is the "end"? Are you letting yourself believe the myths you might have heard about what happens in menopause?
2. Have you gained information from books, doctors, and so on that has been helpful in understanding just what might happen?
3. Have you shared your knowledge, fears, anxieties, and doubts with your partner?
4. Are you letting yourself accept the fact that menopause is just another event in the natural process of life—a chance for more growth?
5. Did you know that men go through a menopausal phase? Have you and your partner discussed it? Have you learned anything about male menopause to help him?

Coming down:
This one is a toughie: consider you are pregnant with a
firstborn. How would you share this experience with your
partner? Would you invite him to listen to the heartbeat?
Go to doctor's visits with you? Would you share the painful
times? Would you even let him see the baby delivered? How
important is your partner to how you feel about your body?
Does he need to know how you feel? Can you share your
concerns about your bodies? Can you touch each other when
you hurt? Menopause should not stop you from sharing
yourselves.

about the authors

Joel Robert Davitz, a graduate of the University of Illinois, received his Ph.D. in psychology from Columbia University. He was a Ford Foundation Fellow and a faculty member at Yale University before becoming a professor in the Psychology department of Teachers College, Columbia University.

Lois Leiderman Davitz, a graduate of the University of Michigan, received her Ph.D. from Columbia University. She was on the faculty of the University of Illinois and the School of General Studies, Columbia University before becoming a Research Associate at Teachers College, Columbia University.

The Davitzes have worked together on various research studies for over twenty-five years and have published extensively in the behavioral sciences.